JN436279

손광현의

유유자적
悠悠自適

나의 사랑하는 아내와 가족, 의학공부를 뒷받침해 주신 어르신,
학문學文과 임상臨床의 가르침을 주신 국내외國內外 스승님들께
이 작은 글 모음을 헌정獻呈합니다.

Korean / English Version

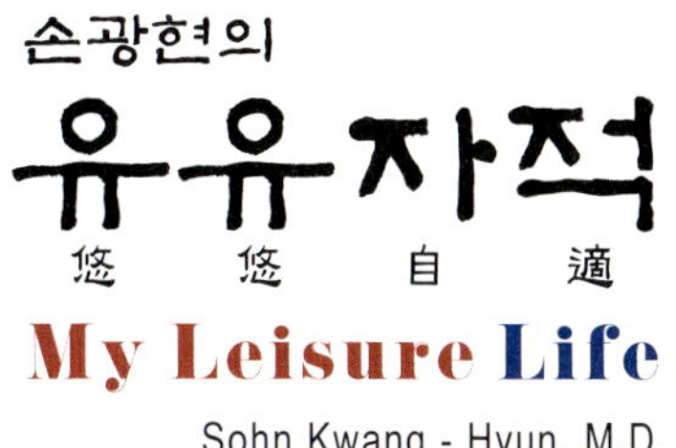

Sohn Kwang - Hyun. M.D.

인지
생략

유유자적(悠悠自適)

2013년 6월 25일 초판 1쇄 발행

지은이 손광현 / **펴낸이** 김재련 / **펴낸곳** 학마을B&M / **기획** 이덕화 / **편집, 디자인** 정명훈
제작 송대규 / **관리** 정대룡 / **전화** 02-324-2993~4, 070-8700-0996 / **팩스** 02-324-2904
홈페이지 www.kookjeon.com / **주소** 서울 마포구 동교동 200-19 오비브빌딩 4층 / **등록번호**
제1-2106호 / ISBN 978-89-87576-93-0(02810) / ⓒ 손광현, 2013, printed in KOREA

가격 10,000원

서언序言과 감사感謝의 말씀

悠悠自適 My Leisure Life의 내용을 엮어보고자한 동기는 단순합니다. 전문직에서 은퇴생활에 들어선 2002년경부터 가끔 써본 글들이 의료전문 주간신문인 〈메디칼 업저버(MO)〉와 〈더 닥터(The Dr)〉에 게재되었습니다. 그 글들 중 일부를 골라 수정 · 보완하여 책으로 묶어보았습니다.

주변의 도움을 받아 영역English version을 시도해 보기도 하고, 작은 모임에서 가끔 읽어보기도 하는 사이에 어느덧 팔순에 들어서게 되어 벗들과 소통도 하고 싶기에 용기를 내어 한글 원문과 영어 번역문의 형태로 글들을 엮어 보았습니다.

정작 글의 내용은 Ⅰ부에서는 은퇴자의 아침으로 시작, Ⅷ부에서는 알파와 오메가적 삶의 대칭의 느낌을, Ⅱ · Ⅲ부에서는 여행과 생활의 현실에서 만난 사실들에 대한 나의 생각을, Ⅳ부에서는 사이언스적 테마를, Ⅴ · Ⅵ · Ⅶ부에서는 자유로운 한 시민의 보편적 인식을 시정詩情 내지는 서정敍情의 형식으로, 더러는 저널Journal의 형식으로 적어보았습니다.

우선 누구보다 적극적으로 시집 출간에 애써 주신 〈메디칼업저버〉 사의 노영수 회장님과 예쁜 시집으로 탈바꿈시켜 주신 학마을B&M의 편집진 여러분께 큰 감사를 드립니다. 아울러 〈메디칼 업저버〉가 우리 의료계의 훌륭한 전문 주간신문으로 계속 성장과 발전이 함께 하시기를 간절히 바랍니다.

영문번역에 관련하여서는 시적 영역의 번역은 일반적으로 난해하다는 것, 저자의 한글 원저가 아직 시 · 서정적 전문인의 경지에 이르기에는 먼 상태일 것임에도 영역자님들께서 큰 이해와 격려로 이를 시도試圖해 주신 점, 또 서로 다른 개성의 번역자들이 함께해 주심에 대하여 큰 감사를 드립니다.

나의 귀중한 번역자님들은 J.W.Chung(Ji Won): ph.D.Candidate, English and Comparative Literary Studies, U.K님, S.G. Hearn(Soo Goon): Reverend, Dr., CA님, J.C. Son(James C.), Mentor, Houston, Texas님, Charlie Maeng(Reporter, ITN. U.K)님들이십니다. 이번 수고에 대하여 큰 감사를 드립니다. 아울러 초기 버전에 참여해 주신 Majorie Kwah, Mira Kim, Ms. Kang님께도 감사드립니다.

나의 사랑하는 아내와 가족, 의학공부를 뒷받침해 주신 어르신, 학문學文과 임상臨床의 가르침을 주신 국내외國內外 스승님들께 이 작은 글 모음을 헌정獻呈합니다. 그간 몸 담아온 직장의 원장님들과 벗들은 평생 나의 삶과 함께하는 가장 소중한 분들임을 항상 인식하며 감사하고 있습니다.

50주년 (한 · 미) 의대동문, 60주년 고교 (한 · 미) 동문 제형 및 열정을 함께 바쳐 온 흉부외과학회의 회원 제위와의 평소의 소통에 대하여 감사의 뜻을 표합니다.

2013년 5월

저자 손 광 현

Preface and Acknowledgement

MY Leisure Life; "The Poetry of Living in Peaceful Retirement"

What led me to write a book about my leisure life is simple. After I retired from my profession in 2002, I started to occasionally write short pieces of work, which were published in two medical newspapers, the Medical Observer and The Dr. While I ventured at producing English versions of my work with the help of the people around me, and while, from time to time, I read my work at small gatherings, I suddenly found myself turning 80. In my desire to communicate with my peers, I plucked up courage to publish a collection of my writings in both korean version and English translation.

The book consists of eight segments: Part 1 starts the book with "A Retiree's Morning" followed by my thoughts on matters I learned through travel and reality in Part 2 and 3. Prat 4 regards scientific themes while in Parts 5 to 7, a free individual's universal perception is shared in poetic, lyrical and journalistic forms. The final Part 8 contains words on the Alpha-Omega symmetry of life.

Special thanks are due to Y. S. Noh, President of the Medical Observer, and J.R. KIM, President of the Hakmaul Books & Media, and their editorial staff to publish this book. I sincerely hope the MO grows to become a valuable medical newspaper in korea.

To share a few words on the English translation, first I would like to acknowledge the general difficulty of translating poetic writing. Second, despite my writing in korean being far from reaching an accomplished poetic level, the translators have shown great understanding and support in their translations. I would like to thank the contribution of all translators whose personal styles differ.

My valued translators whose initials appear at the end of the English versions are J.W.(Ji Won) Chung(ph.D. Candidate, English and Comparative Literary Studies, University of Warwick, U.K.), S.G.(Soo Goon)Hearn (Reverend,Dr., CA), J.C.(James C.)Son, (Mentor, Houston, Texas) and Charlie Maeng(Reporter, ITN, U.K). I am extremely grateful for their work. Thanks to Majorie Kwah, Mira Kim, Ms. Kang there help of initial version.

I would like to dedicate this small collection of writings to my wife, family and parents who supported me through my medical studies, and professors (inside and outside korea) who gave me guidance in both academic and clinical fields. My fellow colleagues and co-workers will remain my dearest friends in my life.

I would also like to thank my friends for the recent 50th (Korea-American) Medical School Alumni and 60th (Korea-American) High School Alumni, along with the members of the Korean Society for Thoracic & Cardiovascular Surgery for continuing to regularly communicate with me.

2013. 5

Kwang Hyun Sohn

Contents

Ⅲ. 나일 강의 단상
The Nile River

Ⅳ. 갈라파고스의 일기
Galapagos Diary

V. 이구아수의 인디언 이야기
Indian Story of Iguassu

VI. 오 오! 대한민국
O! Korea

Ⅶ. 현실은 DNA 갈등
Reality is a DNA discords

Ⅷ. 내려다보니
Looking Back

유유자적悠悠自適
은퇴자의 아침엔 선택의 자유만이 있다

I. 유유자적, 은퇴자의 아침

그대 걸어온 발자국
A Footprint You Made in Walking / Version by, J.W.Chung

유유자적, 은퇴자의 아침
A Contented Retirement / Version by, J.W.Chung

삶이 주는 시
Peotry By Life / Version by, J.W.Chung

시간은 너와 나, 우리들의 벗
Time is You and I, Our Companion / Version by, S.G.Hearn

사회는 언제나 소중한 현실
Society is Always Important Reality / Version by, S.G.Hearn

그대 걸어온 발자국

그대 걸어온 발자국
모래 위에 남긴 발자국
파도는 쉽게 지워버리네

그대 걸어온 발자국
생활 속에 남긴 발자국
사람은 쉽게 잊어버리네

그대 걸어온 발자국
미래 속에 남길 발자국
세상은 쉽게 변해버리네

그대 영원 속에 새겨질 발자국
꿈과 사랑과 진실의 발자국
영원히 간직할 그대만의 발자국

A footprint you made in walking

A footprint you made in walking
Is a foot mark remained yet on the sand
Sea waves wash it away too easily

A footprint you made in walking
Is a foot mark left out in the life
People forget it too readily

A footprint you are to leave behind
Is a foot mark to be reserved for the future
World changes it relentlessly

A footprint you are to engrave in soul
Is a foot mark of dream, love and truth
It is of none but my own, to be kept eternally.

유유자적, 은퇴자의 아침

마음이 풍요로운
은퇴자의 아침이다

스스로 택해 온
오랜 임무에서
경쟁에서 벗어난다

활짝 열린 새장의 문 밖에는
넓은 세상이 있다
자연의 시詩가 있다

자유로운 시간이 있다

가벼운 마음으로
들과 산과 바다를 찾는다

설레는 가슴을 안고
다는 갈 수 없는 먼 곳으로
낯선 눈동자와 문화를 만난다
영감이 가득한 작품과 역사
예술혼 가득한 무대 위의 조화
선율의 재능을 만난다

가끔
명상에 잠긴다.
때론 글을 써 본다

유유자적悠悠自適
은퇴자의 아침엔
선택의 자유만이 있다

A Contended Retirement

This is the morning
Of a contended retired man (with)
an affluent mind

I am free
From duty, From struggle

Outside the wide open cage door
There is the vast world
There is poetry of nature
There is time of companion of mine

Light-heartedly, I head to field,
to mountains, to the ocean

With a beating heart,
I head to far away cities
I relish new eyes, new cultures
Encounting art full of spirit and stories
The performing stage and harmony
I am enraptured by infinite talents

At times,
I journey into the spirit,
I write in passion

A contented retirement

There exists only the freedom of choice
Suiting one's place
This is the morning of a contended retired man.

삶이 주는 시

삶은 바로 오늘 이곳에 있는 것

어제는 이미 지나간 소중함
내일은 끝없는 욕망
오늘의 삶 속에 진실이 있는 것

삶의 현재는 희로애락
생로병사는 삶의 현실

인과응보는 열매처럼
흥망성쇠는 역사처럼 삶과 함께 가는 것

삶이 추구하는 궁극적 경지는
가치의 성취인가
소유의 경쟁인가
쾌락의 충족인가

삶의 오늘, 지금 이곳의 너와 나,
우리의 만남이 가장 소중한 인연인 것
우리의 대화가 가장 귀중한 신뢰인 것
우리의 눈빛이 가장 진정한 사랑인 것

세상은 삶의 보고寶庫
빛이 있는 오늘의 삶을
함께 하리, 균형 하리, 긍정 하리라

그리고 언제 어디서든
하늘이 주는 선물을 감사히 받으리라

삶이 주는 시詩를 담담히 읊으리라

Poetry by Life

Life, here and now

Yesterday, preciousness past
Tomorrow, desire unbounded
Truth is in life today

Present life is joy, anger, sorrow, pleasure
Men's sufferings reality
Men's nemesis like the fruit
Men's vicissitudes like history, pass with life

Is life's ultimate pursuit
Creation of worth
Competition for possession
Fulfillment of happiness

You and me, now and here,
Our union is the fate,
Our talks the sincerest faith,
Our gauge the truest love

The world is life's memoir
I shall nurture whole heartedly today's radiant life
Be together, be balancing, be positive

And
Wherever, Whenever,
Shall I gratefully accept Heaven's gifts

I shall sing joyfully life's poetry.

시간은 나의 벗, 우리들의 벗

시간은 나의 벗, 우리들의 벗
한 뼘 인생을 시간으로 그려 본다

자라고 배우고 일 배우며 각각 10년
성숙하고 결실하고 수확하며 각각 10년
은퇴하며 유유자적하며 복지의 10년까지

저마다의 삶은 천차만별

시간은 너와 나, 우리들의 벗,

저마다의 시간에 얽매여 산다
저마다의 시간을 창조하며 산다

시간은 영원히 흐르는 자연 속의 숫자
시간은 가능성 다양성의 물리
시간은 때로는 빅뱅을 낳는 기적의 괴물?

시간은 하늘이 내리는 공평한 선물

시간은 모든 것을 초월하는 삶의 가치

시간은 나의 벗, 우리들의 벗

Time is a companion of mine, Our companion

Time is a companion of mine, Our companion
Ponder a short span of life as time

Growing up, learning and pursuing a trade,
A decade for each,
Maturing, fructifying and harvesting,
A decade for each,
Retiring, living in serene blissfulness,
And even a tranquility for a decade each

An infinite variety of time spent by everyone
is manifold in character and number,

Time is 'you and I', our companion

Oneself is surviving slaving to time,
Oneself is surviving creating time for themselves

Time is an unceasing number amid nature
Time is a possibility of diversity amid physically
Time is an occasional 'big-bang' that begets
a miraculous monster?

Time is a God-given impartial gift!

Time is treasure much more treasurable than
a golden nugget of everyone's worthiness

Time is a companion of mine, Our companion.

사회는 언제나 소중한 현실

젊음은 아름다움,
경이로움
역동의 계절

욕망과 성장과 인고로
역사는 어느새
환갑還甲
그리고 육십육
성숙의 계절
수확의 계절

역할과 권위, 책임과 가치는
은퇴의 품위
은발의 매력

고희古稀와 희수喜壽에도
사회는 엄연한 현실
삶의 고유함 다양함을
다듬으면 황금의 계절

팔순八旬에도 미수米壽에도
사회는 소중한 현실
걸어온 발자국을
담담히 새기면 회고의 계절

백수白壽엔 미소, 천수天壽는 꿈

사회는 언제나 소중한 현실
현실은, 자신의 (선택인) 것

선택은 자유인 것

The Society is Always the Precious Reality

Youth is a beauty and wonderment , and
It is a season of physical vigor

With desire, growth and durability,
The history is being made before one
acknowledges it
The ages of diamond jublilee and sixty six
A season of maturity and
A season of harvesting

A social role and authoritarianism, an
accountability and worthiness
Are the elegance of retirement and
The delights of silvery hair

For an age of septuagenarian
A society is a solemn realism
Cultivating, it will become a season of gold

For an age of octogenarian
A society is a precious realism
For the footprints of the days of yore,
if one reflects attentively
It could be a season of reminiscence

A smile for the centurial age,
and a dream for ninety nine
The Society is always the precious reality
The reality is for one to choose

The choice is free for one to choose.

그의 삶의 모든 것, 시대의 모든 것, 인간의 모든 것을 그린다

Ⅱ. 나의 눈에 비친 파리

나의 눈에 비친 파리
Paris Gleaming in My Eyes

뮤제 피카소
Musee Picasso / Version by. J.W.Chung

프라하의 감동
Moved by Prague / Version by. J.W.Chung

베네치아 나의 추억
Venice, My Memory / Version by. C.Maeng

백조가 짝을 지어 날으네
White cranes are flying in pairs

카파도키아의 지하도시는
The Underground City of Cappadocia / Version by. J.C. Son

나의 눈에 비친 파리

날개 아래
묘한 기하학
다이아몬드 도시

사람과
만남들이
부딪치며 시샘하는 도시

추억을 만들어
세느 강물에 흘려보내며
즐거워하는 온갖 사람들의 도시

나의 눈에 비친 파리

Paris gleaming in my eyes

Beneath the wings,
Strange geometry
The diamond city

People
They meet and
Stumble over jealousy in this city

Memories
Floating away on Seine
They are happy in this city

Paris gleaming in my eyes.

뮤제 피카소

뮤제 피카소의 따뜻한 한나절
여행자들 속에 섞여
이상한 그림들과 씨름을 한다

잘 길들여진 고전의 허물을 벗는다
생각의 자유, 표현의 자유, 모더니즘Modernism으로 향한다.
큐비즘Cubism시대를 들어선다
Les Demoiselles d'Avinon(1907), 입체파시대의 초기작품
언젠가 아비뇽에서 기차를 내린 적이 있다

서리얼리즘Surrelism, 이해하기 힘든 그림들
나는 생각을 그린다
"I paint things as I think them, not as I see them."
Woman Running on the Beach(1922),
Le Femme Acrobat(1930),
Woman in the Red Armchair(1932),
한참 때의 값비싼 그림들이 벽을 꽉 채운다

Minotaur(1933) 시리즈, 황소의 머리, 사람의 몸
작가 자신이다. 야수의 욕망이 극대화된다
일곱 여성이 그의 생애를 릴레이하듯 동반한다
천부적 화가의 정력과 탐욕과 예술혼을 증폭시킨다

Guernica(1937)(Madrid Museo Nationale 소장),
전쟁의 고통과 죽음의 바다…
Massacre in Korea(1951), 선과 악을 그린다
옛, 뉴욕과 서울의 전시회를 기억하며 간다

20세기의 그는 프로이드(1900), 1차세계대전(1914-8),
러시아혁명(1919), 히틀러 총통(1933), 스페인전쟁(1936-9),
2차세계대전(1939-45)과 원자탄, 한국동란, 월남 전쟁,
인류의 달 착륙(1969) 등 세계사와 함께 산다

그의 삶의 모든 것, 시대의 모든 것,
인간의 모든 것을 그린다

Musee Picasso

A mild day at Musee Picasso
Mingled with tourists
I tackle strange drawings

Cast off the skin of well accustomed classics
Head toward liberal thoughts,
liberal expression and Modernism.
Enter the age of Cubism
'Les Demoiselles d'Avinon'(1907)?
an early work of Cubism
I've unboarded a train once in Avinon

Surrealism? works hard to understand
"I paint things as I think them, not as I see them,"
'Woman Running on the Beach'(1922)
'Le Femme Acrobat'(1930)
'Woman in the Red Armchair'(1932)
Priceless works fill the walls

The 'Minotaur'(1933) series?
bull's head, man's body
The artist himself. The beast's passion maximized

Seven women as if relaying his life, accompany him
The artist's inborn vitality,
greed and artistic spirit are amplified

'Guernica'(1937)(Madrid Museo National)
Sea of war's agony and death
'Massacred in korea'(1951), ? a portrayal of good and evil
I pass by as exhibitions in New York and Seoul come to mind

A 20th century man, he lives with world history?
Freud(1900), World War I(1914-8), Russian Revolution(1919)
Hitler(1933), Spanish Civil War(1936-9), World War Ⅱ (1939-45)
and the nuclear bombing, Korean War, Vietnam War,
Man's landing on the moon(1969)

Pablo Picasso (1881-1973) ? painter, sculpture
He portrays everything in life, in time, and in man.

프라하의 감동

일찍이 비세리드Vysehrad 언덕에
보헤미안이 정착(6C)하더니
프라하 성Prague Castle을 짓고(870's)
나라를 세운다.
이곳 성 비투스 성당St. Vitus Cathedral 종탑에 서면
도심을 껴안고 넘쳐흐르는 블타바Vltava 강을 본다

체코Czech 1,000년의 역사, 근세의 이야기
1·2차 대전, 전후의 소용돌이 속에
프라하의 봄(Prague Spring, 1968)
벨벳혁명(Velvet Revolution, 1989)의
감격을 겪는다

고궁의 돌길 여기저기에선
꽉 짜인 콘서트 프로그램으로
붐비는 여행자들의 발길을 유혹한다

성 조지 성당St. George's Basilica에서의 한나절
수직으로 치켜든 바이올린의 활이
지휘봉 그 자체인 보헤미안 연주자,

내려켜는 모차르트, 구노의 꽉 차는 음율,
드보르작 블타바 나의 조국Vltava My Father land엔
끊일 줄 모르는 감동의 박수를 보낸다

양쪽으로 동상, 조각상이 늘어선
찰스 다리(Charles Bridge, 1358)는
흥겨운 악사들의 다리
만남의 다리, 우정의 다리
군중들은 화가의 모델이 된다

저녁이면 천하일품, 고성의 야경
둘이서 꼭 쥐고 머물러 있고 싶은 다리
짧은 여정의 '프라하Praha의 감동'

Moved by Prague

Long ago on Hill Vysehrad
Settled the Bohemians (6C),
Built the Prague Castle (870' s)
And founded a country
Standing on St. Vitus Cathedral's bell tower
I look down on River Vltava flowing around the city's center

One thousand years of Czech history, a story of modern age;
In the gulf of World War 1 and 2,
Prague Spring(1968)
Velvet Revolution(1989)
Inspire the visitor

Along the old castle's stone path,
Full concert programs
Tempt the crowded traveler's path

Half a day at St. George's Basilica;
The violin bow lifted toward the sky,
Is itself the Bohemian musician's baton,
Playing Mozart, Gounod's rich rhythm

To Dvorjak's 'Vltava My Fatherland'
Given are endless applauds

Lined with statues on both side,
Charles Bridge(1358)
Is the bridge of merry musicians
The bridge of encounter, the bridge of friendship
Crowds become the painter's model

At night, splendid is the old castle night view
Wishing to stay on the bridge hand-in-hand
Moved am I by the short journey at Prague.

베네치아 나의 추억

산 마르코 광장 주변을
맴돌고 나서

느긋하게 끝내는 디너 테이블에
마주앉아 재잘대는 동안
이곳저곳에서 튀어나와
불러대기 시작하는 즉석 오페라 꾼들
몰려드는 인파의 박수만으로도 충분한 흥행
한밤이 지나도록 그칠 줄을 모른다

곤돌라에 몸을 싣고 철썩대며
괴테가 묵고 간 곳
셰익스피어 작품 속 무대를 지난다
대를 이어가는 재능
불어서 만드는 유리공장, 진열장 속 작품들
영혼들만 누워 있는 작은 섬, 수도원 묘지를 간다

9월 초 그랜드 커널의 리개터는 장관이다
여기저기 왕실 손님들이 빤히 보이는 자리
초대해준 어느 귀족 후예의
발코니에 앉아 구경하며
베네치아의 꿈 이야기를 듣는다

학회가 끝나던 어느 저녁 파티,
넘치는 손님들로 붐벼대는 볼룸
물 속에 세워진 돌기둥이
무게를 견뎌낼까 괜히 걱정이다

묘한 것은
작은 공간에서 부딪치는 만남들이
더욱 더 다정하다는 것
베네치아, 나의 추억

Venice, My Memory

I wondered around San Marco square

At the closing dinner table
chat with each others
who appeared from here and there
the opera mania starts singing
With the gathered crowds' clap
at the successful performance
that never stopped all through the night

I ride in the gondola
where Goethe stayed
passed by the stage in for Shakespeare's works
inherited talent
At a glass factory made from blowing
works on display,
I see a small island where souls lie
stop by monastery cemetery

In early September,
miraculous Regater in grand canal
I look at the royal household guests easily
invited to the peer's balcony
watch and hear Benecia's dream

Some dinner party after seminar
crowded with guests in the ball room
The stone wall built in the water
worry about its collapse

Queer one,
meeting in the small space
more emotional
Venice, My memory.

백조가 짝을 지어 날으네

백조가 짝을 지어 날으네
굽이굽이 단풍 사이로

사뿐히 내려앉네
노학동 언덕 위에

한발 두발
천천히 걸어가네
황금빛 논두렁을

먹이를 찾는지
벗을 기다리는지

그림을 그리는지

White cranes are flying in pairs

White cranes are flying in pairs,
Winding through autumnal tints;

And they land with their feathers
Lightly on the hill of Nohakdong

Step by step, they wander
Through the golden rice fields,

Looking for food,
Seeking out friends,

Drawing a picture.

카파도키아의 지하도시는

카파도키아의 지하도시는
무거운 침묵의 여행이었다

신앙을 순교한 흔적이었다
고난을 극복한 흔적이었다
지혜로 생존한 흔적이었다
소망을 기도한 흔적이었다

가이드의 설명만 또박또박 이어질 뿐,

어둠 속으로
한줄기 빛이
지하 8층 우물바닥 깊숙이까지 비치었다

빛은 생명만큼 소중한 염원

침묵 속에서
할렐루야가
마주치는 사람들의 눈동자마다
가득하였다

카파도키아의
케이마크리, 데린쿠유
미로의 지하도시는
무거운 추억의 여행이었다

The Underground City of Cappadocia

To walk through cave cities of Cappadocia
was a journey of solemn silence

It was-
The trace of martyrdom for faith,
The mark of overcoming difficulties,
The survival by wisdom,
The indication of player's for hope

In darkness,
a ray of the sun
shone through,
to the deep bottom
of the eighth floor underground well

Light is one's heart's desire as dear as life···

In silence,
'Halleluiah'···
Not a soul was to be seen,
without the acclamation
in the eyes

Of Cappadocia-
Kaymakli,
Derinkuyu,
Underground city in a maze ···
All is left
for a trip of solemn memory.

사각사각 발걸음 소리엔 아무런 두려움도 아무런 부끄럼도 없다

Ⅲ. 나일 강의 단상

나일 강의 단상
The Nile River / Version by, S.G. Hearn

앙코르 와트 앙코르 톰
Angkor Wat, Angkor Thom / Version by, J.W.Chung

로도스 섬의 해변엔
Seashore in Rhodos Island / Version by, C.Maeng

미움은 미움을 낳고
Love and Hate / Version by, J.W. Chung

셰익스피어 생가에서
Shakespeare House / Version by, J.W. Chung

나일 강의 단상 -피라미드의 위용-

흐르는 시대의 물결
흐르는 나일Nile 강의 물결

5,000년 이집트 역사 - 고대 문명의 발상지
초기, 중기, 신왕조, 후기에 이르는 BC원년 근처까지 거슬러 가본다

크고 작은 파라오Pharaoh들의 욕망의 흔적;
기자Ghiza의 피라미드Pyramids와 스핑크스Sphinx의 위용
그 건축의 기초, 기하학의 경이로움부터 만나며 발걸음을 시작한다
아부 심벨Abu Simbel, 아스완Aswan, 룩소르Luxor
연변의 거대한 신전들의 벽마다 기둥마다에
가득히 새겨진 상형문자象形文字와 파피루스Papyrus의
불가사의에 흠뻑 취해본다

찬란했던 왕조들의 수 천 년- 메네스Menes, 쿠푸Khufu,
투탄카문Tutankhamun, 람세스Ramses왕들의 유적-
왕들의 계곡King's Valley을 거쳐 카르낙Karnak 신전
오벨리스크Obelisk의 위용을 앵글에 담아본다

그들의 삶과 사회, 죽음 그리고 사후세계까지-
사려 깊은 장례와 미라, 회생回生의 신념
그들의 신神과 태양, 사막의 오아시스Oasis
양과 코브라와 자칼의 이야기 틥 속에
상상의 날개를 펼쳐 본다

역사의 속성은 흥망성쇠-
고대 이집트는 알렉산더Alexander-프토레미Ptolemy왕조
안토니Antony-클레오파트라Cleopatra의 죽음으로 이어지며
옥타비안Octavian 로마Roma의 지배로 넘어간다
A.DAnno Domini 시대의 물결로 흘러간다

요동치는 엄연한 현실의 알렉산드리아, 카이로Cairo
나일 강 삼각주를 내려다보며 돌아오는 일정
고대와 현대가 공존하는 공간, 문명의 발상지
이집트의 미래를 단상斷想해본다

The Nile River

Epochal streaming wave
Streaming river of Nile
Five chiliads of Egyptian history – the cradle of ancient civilization
Incipiency, metaphase, dynasties, and treading back near to the first year Before Christ(B.C)

Big and small traces of Pharaoh's ambitions,
Giza's pyramids and the majestics of the Sphinx,
From the beginning of that construction, the wonderment of its geometry
Meeting them as I troded every step
Abu Simbel, Aswan Dam, Luxor –
Along the river Nile, the walls and the pillars of the gigantic shrine,
Engraved in hieroglyphics, and
I am deeply being intoxicated with the wonders of papyrus.

Brilliant dynasties throughout the number of chiliads –
Menes, Khufu,
Tutankhamun, Ramses and their remains –
Through the valley of Kings, Karnak's majestic Obelisk shrine gets caught in the angle

Their lives and society, death and thereafter -
Thoughtful funerals and mummy, conviction of reanimation
Their gods and sun, oasis of desert, sheep and cobra, wamings of scorpions,
My imagination is spreading widely

A brief course of history is risen and demised,
Ancient Egypt was Alexander - Ptolemy dynasty,
Continuing with the death of Antonius-Cleopatra, and
surpassing over to Octavian Augustus of Rome's rule
Streaming down the epoch of the Anno Domini

Solemnly but realistic Alexanrian shake, Cairo,
On retuming, overlooking the Nile's delta,
It's a coexisting spatial moment betwixt the old and new,
Fragmentating the origin and the future civilization of Egypt.

앙코르 와트 앙코르 톰

저마다 다른 눈을 가진
온갖 고장의 사람들이
함께 앉아
어둠을 걷어내는
앙코르 와트Angkor Wat의
해맞이를 한다

기氣가 사라진
망각의 문명
온통 영광의 유적만이 남아 있다

흥망의 역사, 성쇠의 잔해가
빛을 받는 아침이다

신비의 부드러움으로 낮과 밤을 지키는
앙코르 톰Ankor Thom, 바이온Bayon의
창조의 신 브라마Brahma 사면 상
사랑과 파괴의 신 시바Shiva
미소와 춤의 신 압사라Apsara
가득히 벽을 메꾼 신들에 둘러싸여
힌두Hindu가 오가며 붓다Buddha와 공존한다

나무관세음보살

살아 숨쉬는
폐허 속 크메르Khmer의 위대한 예술
글귀마저 흩어지는 앙코르의
천년을 거슬러 찾는다

영원한 것은
흐르는 시간뿐
오늘도 어김없이 해는
신비의 사원 서편으로 지고 있다

Angkor Wat, Angkor Thom

Different Colored-eye people
From various places
Gather around to
Greet the sun
At Angkor Wat
Dismissing the darkness

Spirits vanished
In civilization of oblivion,
Only the ruins of glory remain.
History of fortunes, ashes of destinies
Receive the morning light

With mysterious gentleness guarding
Bayon Angkor Thom's
God of creation Brahma,
God of love and destruction Shiva,
Spirit of smile and dance Apsara,
Surrounded by divinities crowning the walls
Hinduism and Buddism coexist

Avalokitesvara God of Mercy

Breathing its life,
Khmer's great art in ruins
Trace back Angkor's thousand years
Where even words fall apart.

Eternity
Is passing time alone;
Today, doubtless,
To the west of the mysterious temples.

로도스 섬의 해변엔

로도스 섬의 해변엔
파도와 자갈이 만드는
속삭임이 있다

구릿빛 곡선과 선글라스 만의
침묵의 구역이 있다

사각사각 발걸음 소리엔
아무런 두려움도
아무런 부끄럼도 없다

수정 같은 푸른 에게 해의
미풍이 불어올 땐
무아無我에 몰입하는
영혼靈魂만이 있다
뮤즈 신, 에우테루페 여신들의
욕망의 신화神話만이 있다

선글라스 속 시선이 교차하는
짜릿한 순간의
현실現實만이 박동搏動한다

로도스 섬의 해변엔
자연과 영혼과 현실의
속삭임이 있다

Seashore in Rhodos Island

At the seashore of Rhodos Island
waves and pebbles made whispered

In sun-tan colored curve and sun-glass
a silence exists

I hear the sound of light footsteps
not frightened
and feel no shyness

like blue crystal
From the Agean seashore
whenever breeze blows
I fall into ecstasy
There, only souls exist
Muse god, desire legend of Euterupe godess

where with her eyes crossed in sunglasses
in a thrilling moment
Reality beats

On Rhodos Island
Nature, soul and reality whisper.

미움은 미움을 낳고

미움은 미움을 낳고
불화를 낳고
파괴를 낳고
역사에 상처만 남기네

사랑은 사랑을 낳고
평화를 낳고
창조를 낳고
역사에 꽃을 피우네

사랑과 미움은
서로 부둥켜안고 씨름하며
때로는 아름답게
때로는 처절하게
온갖 삶의 흔적을
가정과 사회와 역사의
무대 위에 연출하네

돌이켜보면
사랑도 미움도
모두
너와 내가
스스로 택해서 만든
각본인 것을

미움은 무서운 것
사랑은 어려운 것
미래의 무대 위에 연출할
각본은 선택인 것
선택은 용기인 것

Love and Hate

Hate bears hate,
Discord,
Destruction,
And leaves nothing but wound in history

Love bears love,
Peace,
Creation,
And makes history bloom

Love and hate
Wrestling each other,
Sometimes beautifully,
Sometimes miserably
Present on stage
Of family, society and history,
All traces of life

Looking back,
Love and hate,
Both
Are scripts
You and I
Ourselves made

Hate is dreadful,
Love is difficult
Chosen is the script
To be presented on future's stage
The choice is courage.

셰익스피어 생가에서

셰익스피어 생가에 가까워질수록
점점 더 궁금해진 것은;
어떻게 인간의 생각을 그처럼 잘 쓰고 다듬었기에
모든 언어와 시대를 초월하여 공감케 하는가?

어려워 말고, 그의 생애의 흔적에 들어서 봐야지
1564년 4월 26일 출생한 그의 성장과정엔 이론異論도 많다
8년 위인 '해사웨이' 와 19세에 결혼을 한다
정원의 나무와 침실과 부엌과 진열품들에 몰려 사진을 찍는다

작가에 대해 공론이 많을수록, 작품은 더 위대해 진다
얼마나 많은 젊음이 '로미오와 줄리엣' 의 사랑에 우는가
얼마나 많은 관객이 '햄릿' 의 비극을 탄식하는가
얼마나 많은 사람이 '그대가 좋을 대로' 삶을 꾸미는가
얼마나 짜릿한 환희를 '한 여름밤의 꿈' 은 잉태하는가
얼마나 무서운 야망과 모략을 '시저' 의 무대는 연기하는가
얼마나 신랄한 집착을 '베니스의 상인' 은 고집하는가
많은 '바드' 의 희극과 '소네트' 는 시샘을 받는다

은퇴 후 고향 '스트라트훠드' 에서 말년을 지낸다
1616년 4월 25일 교회묘소에 삶을 마감한다
축제장 같은 생가 한마당을 떠나면서,
그가 다녔다는 옛 초등학교가 400년이 지난
지금도 그 자리인 것을 본다

돌아오는 길, 푸른 초원을 바라보면서
더욱 더 궁금해진 것은; 누가 더 이상
삶의 감성과 이성을 그처럼 절실하게,
잘 다듬을 수가 있을까? 곰곰이 생각해 본다

셰익스피어의 고전은 인류의 문화재라고 …

Shakespeare House

As I approach Shakespeare's house
I begin to wonder, what makes him
Write, speak, and present man's thoughts
That transcends all languages and time?

Unreservedly, I enter his stage of life,
Born April 26th 1564, many theories about his growth
Marries eight years older Hathaway in the age of 19
In flurry I take pictures of garden trees,
bedroom, kitchen and displays

Many arguments about the writer make his works greater
How many youths cry for Romeo and Juliet's love?
How many viewers lament over Hamlet's tragedy?
How many people dream for the life in As You Like It?
What tingling joy A Midsummer Night's Dream impregnates
What horrible ambition Julius Caesar performs
What obsession The Merchant of Venice insists on
Jealousy the bard's comedies and sonnets receive

He spends his later life in his hometown Stratford-upon-Avon
His life ends April 25th 1616 at a graveyard
As I leave his life of festivals, I see his primary school
400 years later, standing there as it would had

Leaving, as I look at the green plains
A question comes to mind?
Who can carve life's sensibility and reason
Keenly as he did? I fall deep in thought
Shakespeare's classics are humanity's cultural heritages.

인류는 진정 진화進化의 산물인가? 창조의 산물인가?

Ⅳ. 갈라파고스의 일기

갈라파고스의 일기
Galapagos Diary / Version by, J.W. Chung

새로운 패러다임, 프랙탈 이론
New Paradigm, Fractal Theory / Version by, J.W. Chung

뇌 기능이 궁금하다
Curious About Brain Function / Version by, J.W. Chung

호메오스타시스
Homeostasis / Version by, J.C. Son

오브제 2007
Object 2007 / Version by, J.C. Son

갈라파고스의 일기

갈라파고스 섬의 평원에 내려서 보니
안데스 산맥의 고원에서보다 숨 쉬기가 편하다
낮은 곳에 길들여져 있음이 분명하네

산타크루즈 섬의 곳곳에 서있는 선인장
깍뚜스Cactus 명패에는 100세도 200세도 넘는다 적혀 있으니
장수 식물 종種의 표본임이 확실하네

찰스 다윈 연구소에 사육중인
또토스Tortoise는 120세가 되었다 하니
고대 종의 보존임이 증명되네

해변가 곳곳 레스토랑 주변의
이구아나Iguana는 꽤나 못 생긴 첫 인상이더니
며칠 새 그 천진난만함에 어느덧 다정한 벗이 되네

아욜라Ayola 항구로 오가는 뱃길 옆 바위 틈새에는
씨 라이온Sea lion 들이 늘어지게 낮잠을 자니
오랜 파도로 조각된 암벽 콘도의 주인이 따로 없네

핀치Finch베이 비치의 짹짹대는 핀치 되새들은
나와 아내의 식탁 위 메뉴를 함께 즐기니
생물 종과 공존共存하는 평화를 만끽하네

공중에서 바다로 쏜살같이 잠수하는
펠리칸Pelican 새는 낚아챈 고기와 물로
풍선처럼 늘어난 목을 배수排水하니
물새와 물고기의 약육강식弱肉强食이 뚜렷하네

엥겔마이어 포인트의 이곳
최초의 섬 입주자의 부인은
실어증 남편을 극진히 보살피며
늘어나는 섬사람들로 인한
스트레스가 그의 병의 원인이라 늘어놓네

태평양 동쪽 끝, 적도 밑, 갈라파고스 섬들의
자연환경에선 지금도 온갖 생명체 종들의 후손과
그 자손들이 대代를 이어가며
오랫동안 생존경쟁, 자연선택, 적자생존, 변이變異의
진화가 계속되네

호모사피엔스(1868), 인류 종 이후에도
호모에렉투스(1891), 북경원인(1907),
오스트랄로피테쿠스 아프리카누스(1924) 화석化石이
계속 발견되니
〈종의 기원〉 인류는 진정 진화進化의 산물인가?
창조의 산물인가?

Galapagos Diary

Standing on Galapagos plain,
easier it is to breathe than on Andes plateau,
Clearly the road is made on a lower place

Cactuses standing here and there on Santa Cruz Island;
the nameplates show
they are over 100, 200, 300 years old
Plainly they are specimens of long-living plants

A tortoise being bred
at Charles Darwin Research Station is 120 years old
Proven is the preservation of ancient species

Iguana at beaches and restaurants
seemed ugly at first
But in time, their simplicity becomes affectionate friends

In-between rock walls along the waterway
going in and out of Puerto Ayola,
leisurely sea lions take naps
No particular owner has the cliff condo sculptured
by ages of waves
Sparrows chirping at Finch Bay Beach

enjoy the menu on me and my wife's table,
I relish the peace coexisting with living species

The pelican diving like an arrow into the water
boasting its stretched bill
fills itself with fish and water
Clear are the prey and the strong of water birds and fish

East end of Pacific, below the equator,
At Galapagos Islands' natural environment, still
descendants of all kinds of living creatures
carry on family lines, For ages, continue
the struggle for life, choice of nature, survival of the fittest,
and evolution of transition

After the discovery of Homosapiens the species(1868),
on the six continents,
fossils of Homoerectus(1891), Peking Man(1907),
Australopithecus Africanus(1924)
continue to be unearthed
<Origin of the Species>
Is mankind truly the creature of evolution?
The product of creation?

새로운 패러다임, 프랙탈적 이론

곳곳에서
새로운 패러다임이 열린다

한 시대를 지배하던 크고 작은 이론들은
디지털적 세계화의 물결을 타고
역사의 바다 속으로 포용包容된다

자연 속 프랙탈적 카오스적 현상들은
수학의 도전을 낳고 프랙탈적 이론을 낳는다

시간의 단위- 1초에서 100년까지,
그 다정한 유한有限의 인식은 무한無限으로,
무한소小, 무한대大를 넘나든다

크기 · 질량 · 거리와 속도 · 중력 등에 대한
고전古典적 이해理解는
운동, 에너지, 기상현상, 지진, 유전자,
뇌 기능과 우주의 영역에 이르면서
프랙탈적 복잡계複雜系의 무질서無秩序 속
질서와 조화의 신비를 만난다
예측 불가능한 변수變數들에 부딪친다

시장市場과 사회와 정치활동에서마저
불확실성의 해법을 프랙탈적 사고로 접근한다
실용은 보수와 진보를 넘나들고
컴퓨터는 점점 불가능을 가능케 한다

삶의 내일은, 진정
혼돈混沌의 미래일까
자유도度의 미래일까,
그래도 하루해가 뜨고 지는 것만은 확실하다

새로운 패러다임은
새로운 세계를 낳는다

New Paradigm, Fractal Theory

Here and there
new paradigms are on the scene

Diverse theories of big and small-dominant over all others
in an age-riding on the waves of digitalized globalization,
are being tolerated into the sea of the history of the world

New theories
give birth to new paradigms
Fractal and chaos phenomenon in Nature, give birth
to the challenge of mathematics and fractal theories

The concept of time from one second to one hundred years-
that familiar awareness travels from the finite to the infinite,
into each other of the infinitesimal and the infinite, the notion
frequents back and forth

The classic understanding of
size, mass, distance and speed, and gravity,
as applied to kinetic energy, meteorological phenomenon,
earthquake, gene, brain function, and space domain,

meets in a complexity of the fractal system–
the order out of disorder and mystery of harmony
It is confronted by variables beyond estimates

Not excluded are stocks–market, social and political activities,
unpredictable solutions are sought by fractal thinking
Practicalism overrules conservatism and progressivism
Computers make an impossible a possible

Could the tomorrow of living be
the future of confusion,
or the future of free bounds,
But, the sun rises and falls each day

New paradigms give birth to a new world.

뇌 기능이 궁금하다

처마 끝 새장 안에 예쁜 새가 있다
잠시 후 새장 안엔 작은 구렁이가 있다
오빠 새가 구렁이가 되었어

변화를 보고 놀란 동생이 있다
약육강식 상황을 연상할 수 있다
두 개가 하나 속에 공존하는구나,
구렁이는 좋은 단백질과 칼로리로
새 에너지를 만드는구나의 논리도 있다

사람의 대뇌피질엔 10^{11}(1천억)개,
소뇌피질엔 10^{12}(1조)개의 신경 세포가 있다
세포마다 많게는 1만개의 시냅스synapse 즉,
10^{15}(1천조 추정)의 뉴런(신호체계) 사이의 틈이 있다
여기엔 신비의 신경전달 물질들(100종류?)이 분비된다

이 세포 간 활동회로의 대화 기능이 생각을 만든다고?
몸과 마음의 기능을 모니터하고 조절한다고?
뇌 기능은 전기 에너지화되어 뇌파로도 측정된다
좌 · 우뇌의 기능은 다르고 교차되어 말초신경을 지배한다

뇌의 세상만사를 보고, 듣고, 느끼고, 인식하고, 반응한다
요사스럽기까지 한 감정은 희로애락 한다
나로 여겨지는 자아마다 뇌 기능의 활동양상이 다르다
마음은 자유롭고 상상은 무한하다. 의지는 수시로 변한다
생각하고, 기억도 하고, 망각도 하고, 집중하고, 창조도 한다

컴퓨터, 로봇은 정직하기만 하다. 망각도 융통성도 없다
인간은 갖은 욕망을 다 추구한다. 진 · 선 · 미도 추구한다
그래도 일생동안 잠재된 뇌 기능의 10% 정도만 쓴단다
말하고, 쓰고, 그리고 행위하고, 싸움하는 데도…
뇌는 천재도 반대도 만든다. 뇌는 활용할수록 진화한다

인류는 엄청난 역사와, 문화와 과학을 낳았다
성서도, 연꽃 같이 초연한 경전도 낳았다
인간은 영적 존재인가? 영혼靈魂은 불멸한가?
신神은 하늘에 있는가? 마음에 있는가?
현대를 사는 사람의 '뇌 기능이 궁금하다'

Curious About Brain Function

Inside the bird cage at the end of the eaves is a lovely bird
A while after inside the cage is a small serpent
Brother, the bird turned a snake

There is a younger sister startled at the change
There is associates the situation with the law of the jungle
There is a thought that two coexists in one
The predator makes a good protein and calories into new energy

In the human cerebral cortex there are 10^{11}(100 billion),
In the cerebellar cortex 10^{12}(1 trillion) nerve cells
In each cell there are at most ten thousand synapses ;
Gaps between, 10^{15}(1000 trillion) neurons(signal system)
Here mysterious, nerve transmission materials(100?) are secreted

Is it true the communicative function of energy circuit
between these cells makes thought possible?
That it monitors and controls various functions of body-mind?
and intersected, controlling the peripheral nerve
The brain function is also converted into electric energy and
measured by brain waves, and computed images as well
Brain recognizes and responds to what we see, hear, feel in life
Fickle emotions are joy, anger, sorrow, pleasure

The brain function's behavior aspects are different in each self
what we call "I"
The mind is free, imagination boundless, The will, capricious.
Thinking, memory, oblivion, concentration, creation, as well

Computers and robots are always honest;,
There is no loss of memory, no flexibility
Humans persue all kinds of desire
They also persue truth, goodness, and beauty
Yet they use only 10% of life's potential brain function
Although they speak, write, act and fight
The brain makes a genius and the contrary
The brain evolves as it is made use

Mankind created enormous history, culture and science.
Also the bible, and scriptures remarkable as the lotus flower.
Are human spiritual beings? Is the spirit immortal?
Is god up there or in here?
I am curious about the brain function of people of today.

호메오스타시스

스스로를 스스로
바로 다스리려는 그런 기능이
사람의 세포와 몸 안엔 있다
호메오스타시스, 생체의 항상성恒常性 유지기능이다

신비스러울 만큼
세포는 세포 내부 환경을 정상으로 유지하기 위하여
세포 외부환경 변화를 조절한다. 적응한다.
인체가 외부기온이 떨어지면 피부의 떨림으로,
기온이 높아지면 땀으로 열 조절한다

대사과정의 에너지원인 혈당의 정상치 유지는
간 뇌하수체 췌장의 인슐린 분비로 조절한다
혈중 수분 염분 이온 페하(pH) 농도의 변화는
혈액 림프계 콩팥의 배설 기능의 협동으로 조절한다
생리적 화학적 삼투압기전으로 조절한다

인체가 외부로부터 바이러스나 세균의 침습이 있으면
자극의 수신-전달-반응의 피드백 기능으로
백혈구와 면역체계를 동원하여 이에 방어 대응한다
실패하면 질병이 된다. 치료를 받아야한다
자극과 스트레스를 극복하면 노름Norm을 되찾는다

생태계에도 호메오스타시스가;
스스로를 균형하고 자정하고 조정하려는 경향이 있다
인구의 출생과 사망, 식량과 식수, 산업과 공해에서도,
동 · 식물계의 자정작용, 쓰나미 · 엘리뇨 현상에서도,
생태적 · 물리적 힘의 균형을 유지하려는 섭리가? 있다

삶의 현실엔 왜? 세계는 전쟁하는가?
사회는, 인간은 갈등하는가?
웰빙Well-being은 스스로 뿌린 씨앗의 거둠인 것
찾아야 할 지켜야 할, '호메오스타시스'
인간에겐 스스로를 스스로
바로 다스리려는 소망이? 있다

Homeostasis

Being Self by Self,
A cell in a living body has a function to keep itself fit
by proper way of self regulation and maintenance
Homeostasis, an ability to maintain stable condition of the body

Mysterious enough;
The Cell controls changes occurring in its external environment
to keep its internal condition to its best. It adapts itself to
changes
Human body automatically thermo-regulates as outside
temperature drops
by shivering of skin, and by sweat as the temperature goes up

The ideal level of blood sugar for metabolic process is
maintained
by synthesis and release of insulin from liver-pituitary-pancreas
Proper water level, sodium, ions and pH concentration in the
blood are
all regulated in unison by the excretory function of kidney and
so on,
By physiological, chemical and osmosis functions
If body is attacked by viruses or bacteria from outside,

By applying receptor-messenger-reactor feedback function, the white cell
and the immune system are mobilized to react in defence
Defeat and win, the health is restored. The Norm is reclaimed
If fail with the stimuli, the disease develops. Treatment is needed

In ecological system, Homeostasis? is a major issue in the preservation
of self-balancing, self-cleansing, and self-adjusting;
the birth and death rates of population, food and drinking water,
industrial-environmental, self-cleansing inherent in animal kingdom
and vegetable world, global tsunami and El Nino phenomenon …
Are there preservation of ecological and physical balance?
The force of dispensation?

Moreover, There are realities on the scene of life, War,
Social trouble, Individual hatreds going on?
Well-being is a harvesting the seed sown by man himself
'Homeostasis' is here and ready to be much sought after
To man, there is the hope in him to keep himself under control
and maintain himself in proper balance.

오브제 2007

오브제, 그 속에 진실이 있다

흙에 피고 지는 초목, 산과 바다,
태양과 공기와 물과 음양의
조화調和에 대하여, 좀 더
새로운 이치가 밝혀질
새해를 맞는다

미생물과 움직이는 큰 생명체 모두,
생식과 먹이 사슬과 적자생존의
진화進化에 대하여, 좀 더
새로운 해석이 밝혀질
새해를 맞는다

다원적 유전체의 영장류 인간; 영적 존재?,
이기 · 욕망 · 경쟁 · 창의 · 선악의
브레인Brain 게임에 대하여, 좀 더
새로운 지혜가 밝혀질
새해를 맞는다

이루어놓은 역사와, 이루어 질 역사,
민족과 국가와 과학과 문명 간 갈등의
미래未來에 대하여, 좀 더
새로운 예측이 밝혀질
새해를 맞는다

국경 없는 환경, 인류와 생명체 모두,
삶의 터전, 지구와 스페이스Space의
변화變化에 대하여 좀 더 숨어 있는
새로운 사실이 밝혀질

오브제Object 2007년
새해를 맞는다

Object 2007

Object, therein lies the truth
Trees and plants grown out of soil bloom and wither;
For the mountains and sea,
about the Sun, the air, and the waters,
about the harmony of Yin and Yang,
More new principles shall be brought to light,
Yea, in the coming of New Year

Object- therein lies the truth
For all microorganism and big living things
that reproduce and strive to stay alive,
and for the evolution of the survival of the fittest,
More enlightened interpretations shall be revealed,
Yea, in this New Year

Object- therein lies the truth
For man of pluralistic heredity-that spiritual being
with selfishness, desire, creativity,
and about the 'brain game' of good and evil,
The world shall be lighted up
with newer wisdom
Yea, in the New Year

Object- therein lies the truth
For the history that has been and that will be,
About the future of human conflict
among people and nations,
and for science and civilization,
Newer fore sights shall be manifested
Yea, in this New Year

Object- therein lies the truth
About the environment without boundaries,
for all of humankind and living things,
and about changes in their living sites,
their globe, their space,
A new wave of changes is about to blow
Yea, in this New Year

More truth that has been hidden
Shall be revealed in the year 2007
Yea, in this year that I welcome.

삶의 무대는 무한無限한 것이며, 삶의 연출은 자유自由로운 것이며,
삶의 기회는 소중所重하고 감사感謝한 것입니다

V. 이구아수의 인디언 이야기

이구아수의 인디언 이야기
Indian Story of Iguassu / Version by, C.Maeng

나는 고양이를 좋아하는데
I like a kitty cat / Version by, S.G. Hearn

피트니스의 경지에선
At Fitness stage / Version by, C.Maeng

주례사 유감
After Thought on My Wedding Message / Version by, J.C.Son

장인의 길
Going beyond the stage of Accomplishment / Version by, J.C.Son

슬픔은 그렇게 이어진다
Sorrow comes after sorrow / Version by, J.C.Son

이구아수의 인디언 이야기

피안彼岸에는 신비의 낙원이
분명코 있으리라

추장의 명령이 떨어지자
쏜살같이 물결을 타고
저어간다

수평선을 바라보는 눈이
기다림에 지쳐서 불안해진다

두 번째, 세 번째, 네 번째
열 번째 인디언 '까누' 도
돌아오지 않는다

수년 후 하류를 건너
수년 전의 피안에 서서 보니
대자연 구석구석에는
정복되지 않는
비밀이 있었다

이구아수 폭포의
악마의 목구멍

장구한 시간, 그
단애斷崖, 굉음轟音, 안개 속 무지개
인디언 시대까지 줌인zoom in한다.

Indian Story of Iguassu

In Pian(opposit shore)
a mysterious paradise was

Reached the moment when chieftain ordered
us to row swiftly

Eyes looking at the horizon
the chieftain is like a sharp eagle,
who is tired of waiting and became uneasy

The second, third, fourth
and tenth Indian canoe
never come back

A few years later,
they crossed the downstream
looked at the Pian in the past,
in every holes and corners of nature
unoccupied secrets lie

Iguas waterfall
is like the throat of the devil
with a long period, precipice, big noisy rainbow in the mist
and Indian period zoom in.

나는 고양이를 좋아하는데

야옹, 야-옹, 두세 번 불러 보면
동공이 마주친다

야-옹 하고 유연하게 다가온다
특별한 텔레파시Telepathy

양미간을 두세 번 쓰다듬어주면
기다렸다는 듯이
사뿐히 올라앉는다
완벽한 밸런스Balance

두세 번 더 쓰다듬어주면
살며시 눈을 감고 포근해 한다
행복한 순간을 꽤나 즐기는구나
사랑스러운 것
기막힌 에고Ego

어쩌면, 그런 네가
쥐만 만나면, 단숨에 쏜살같이
그의 급소를 물어버리느냐
잔인한 것
철저한 공격Attack

쓰다듬던 손길이
미처, 미움으로 이어지기도 전에
야옹 하고, 박차고 달아난다
아무 미련도 없다는 듯이-

내일이면 다시 다가올 것이
구슬놀이에 여념 없을 것이
너, 정말 유별난 것

나는 아직도 고양이를 좋아하는데

I like a kitty cat

Meow, me-ow, calling her a few times,
Her pupil meets my vision.

M-E-O-W, tenderly, she draws near to me
A special telepathy!

Smooth down softly once or twice
On her forehead betwixt the eyebrows,
As if awaited, she jumps onto my lap softly
A flawless balance!

A few times more of tender stroke given,
Fondly, enjoys herself, eyes closed gently
The kitty cat must enjoy a happy moment all to herself
How lovable!
An amazing self-content!

How can you, look so nonchallant one,
Assault your antagonist so swiftly when you see one!
Attacking his crucial point, so mercilessly,
A brutality!
A thorough assailant!

Before my patting hand
Turns into a detestation,
The kitty cat kicks away, meowing
As if no more lingering affection –

You'll return tomorrow, and
You'll be absorbent with marbles,
You, kitty cats are peculiar persona!

I like a kitty cat, still –

피트니스의 경지에선

순간일지라도
심신이 홀가분한
피트니스의 경지에선
홀인원도, 이글도 나올 수 있듯이…
아마추어에서도

언제나 잘 숙련된
심신이 자유로운
피트니스의 경지에선
최상의 퍼포먼스를 성취할 수 있듯이…
프로들의 경우처럼

언제 어디서나 어떤 조건에서나
심신이 완벽한
피트니스의 경지에선
미션 임파서블도 쿵푸도 액션할 수 있듯이…
작품 속의 슈퍼맨들처럼

올림픽, 월드컵의 메달은
심신이 최상인 컨디션
피트니스의 경지에서 만들어지는
관중이 갈망하는 슈퍼스타들의 탄생

인간에겐
대리만족을 추구하는 묘한 심리가 있다
영원히
불가능의 경우를 뛰어넘는
피트니스의 경지 –

슈퍼(초)능력을 추구하는 욕망이 있다

At Fitness stage

Even momentarily,
mentally and physically unencumbered
at the Fitness stage,
a hole in one and Eagle
come true for the amateur

Who is always well skilled,
mentally and physically free
at the fitness stage
He achieved the best performance
like the professionals

Whenever, wherever and whatever,
mentally and physically perfect
at the fitness stage
it is possible for him to act mission impossible and Kungfu
like supermen, in works

Winning Olympic, world cup medals
based on their mentally and physically best conditions
made from that comes from fitness training stage
superstars birth from audiances anxiety

To humanbeings
exist queer psychology to pursuit procurative satisfaction
forever,
jumping over the impossible cases
fitness stage

longing for super ability.

주례사(主禮辭) 유감

혼인서약婚姻誓約! '그 어떠한 경우에도;
기쁠 때나 슬플 때나, 괴로울 때나 아플 때나
항시 사랑하고 존중하며, 어른을 공경하고
진실한 남편과 아내로서의 도리를
다할 것을 서약誓約 합니다' 하였습니다
이에 주례主禮는, 만장하신 내빈을 증인으로 모시고
부부로서의 결혼이 원만히 이루어졌음을 선언宣言 합니다

생물학적 사랑의 본능으로 남녀가 일심동체가 되는 것입니다
사회학적 삶의 역할에서 한 가정이 이루어지는 것입니다
음양의 천생연분으로 결혼이 이루어진 것입니다.

이제, 각각의 유전자로, 각자의 환경 속에서, 각자의 뜻대로
성장해온 독립된 두 개성과 개성의 만남이 행복한 부부,
행복한 가정, 건전한 결혼생활을 추구하는 것입니다
엄청난 노력努力의 과정으로 만들어지는 것입니다

이해利害와 보상의 셈이 아니라
이해理解와 나눔, 협조와 역할,
칭찬과 창조의 과정으로 이루어질 수 있는 것입니다
기쁨은 함께 나눌수록 커지고, 고통은 나눌수록 작아집니다
서로 너무 따지는 부부, 서로 잘난 부부는 갈등이 증폭됩니다
현명한 부부, 지혜로운 부부의 결혼생활은 사랑이 증폭됩니다

삶의 무대는 무한無限한 것이며,
삶의 연출은 자유自由로운 것이며,
삶의 기회는 소중所重하고 감사感謝한 것입니다

"우리는 진실한 사랑의 슬기, 고귀한 소망,
확고한 신념을 키워 나갈 것입니다" 를 다짐 하소서
"두드리라 그러면 열릴 것이다"

"축복과 영광이 가득할 지어다."
이제, 주례主禮는, 둘이 하나가 되어 결혼행진곡에 발맞추어
세상으로 나서는 신랑 신부에게, 하객 모두와 함께
큰 박수를 보낸다

After thoughts on my wedding message

Marriage Vows; It was so pledged, that they:
"in whatever situations- in joy or in sorrow, in troubles or in sickness,
will always love and respect each other, will pay respect to elders,
will always fulfill spousal duties as faithful husband and wife."
I thereupon pronounced: "by this vow, as witnessed by all guests in
presence, this marriage is expected properly, and you are now bound by this marriage to be 'man and wife'."

A man and a woman are being united as one, biologically, socially, and providentially, through matrimonial bond

Leaving inherited heredity, different home environment, and individual growth, behind, the two independent personalities meet together, are create spousal happiness and family happiness
Perfect marriage is the product of enormous endeavor

It is not of summing up gains and losses. But it is from understanding and sharing. It is the result of cooperation and responsibility, the process

gained through praise and efforts
The bigger the joy becomes as it is shared together,
The smaller the pain becomes because of sharing
between prudent spouses, in a wise family, and in the marital life of love

The stage of life is boundless,
The presentation of life is limitless,
and the opportunities of life are priceless and to be thanked for

For us, 'There is the wisdom of true love,'
For us, 'There are high hopes,'
For us, 'There are clear convictions,'. May all these be assured.
"Knock, then the door will be open."

"We coming you there will be the fullness
of blessings and honor of the new life
This officiator sends a big applause to the bride and groom
who march in step into the world in tune with the wedding march.

장인(匠人)의 길

– 스스로의 성취의 경지에 머무르지 않고…

타고난 재능 때문에
한 평생 스스로의 길만을 간다
길고, 고되고, 외로운 수업修業의 길을 간다
흙을 빚는다, 머릿속에 형태를 뜬다,
만들고, 그림 그리고, 쓰고,
명예도, 풍요도 바라지 않는
순수한 마음의 이름까지 새긴다
태양열이라도 만들려는 심정으로
불꽃을 피우고 응시한다
천지신명에게 기도를 한다
거두는 과정 하나하나;
두들겨 보고, 쓰다듬어 보고, 고르고 또 고른다
쓸만한 새끼만을 키우는 호랑이의 심정으로,
험이 있으면 눈물을 머금고 부셔 버린다
세월은 경험을 낳고, 과학을 낳고,
통달의 경지에 이른다
비로소, 작품이
빛을 받는 날을 맞는다
전시장에서, 박물관에서, 도감 속에서,
대대손손 전해지는 가보 속에서,
소장가의 품안에서 사랑을 받는다
민속을 간직한다, 현대를 나타낸다

장인匠人은 장인 서로를 안다;
흙을 빚듯이, 쇠를 두드리는 마음,
돌을, 자개를, 나무를 다듬는 정신을 서로 안다
작품이 지니는 예술혼魂은 시대를 초월한다
스스로의 성취의 경지에 머무르지 않고
타他에게 보람의 가치를 준다
누가 장인의 가는 길에 비단을 깔아주지 않으랴
장인은 인류에게 값진,
문화의 선물을 안겨준다

Going beyond the stage of Accomplishment

For inborn talent, Artisans go beyond themselves
all their life devoted to their given gift
Long, hard, lonesome... is their pursuit of knowledge;
They shape clay, see, and cut forms in their head;
They make, draws, write, even carving their names
Their passion is to burn, to the intensity of
solar heat in the kiln, to burn to blaze, to bake to create
They pray to the gods of heaven and earth.
Each process of ending their works–
gentle beatings, delicate strokes, going through over and over
to carefully choose the perfect pieces…
as tigers' instinct to spare only useful cub,
They leave no room for laxity
They smash the defect to pieces though having tears in their eyes
Experience bears science, and experience bears art
It leads one to become a master of their work
Only after reaching this stage of creation,
there is a day for a piece of work shines with glory
At an exhibition hall, At a museum, In the books,
As an heirloom handed down for generations,

In the bosom of collectors of curious,
The piece of work gains hearts of all

It harbors folklore, tradition, modernism
An artisan knows another artisan by heart,
as they shape clay, beat iron to form, carve stone, nacre, wood…
They know the spirit embedded in each others work
transcends the sense of the times
He does not stop and stay at his own achievements,
But he passes them over to others to appreciate
Let them taste the joy
Who would refuse to lay the silk carpet on their chosen way
for them to walk on, to honor them?
Artisans send their gift to fellow human beings-
For them to enjoy their invaluable piece of art.

슬픔은 그렇게 이어진다

저마다 타고난 시時가 있다
저마다 타고난 명命이 있다

평균수명을 거치는 계절이 되니
하나하나 세상을 떠나는 소식을 만난다
지극히 자연스러운 인간지사인데
이 순간의 마음이 꽤나 편치를 않다

살아 생전에 남긴 다양한 사연만큼이나
크고 작은 발자국만큼이나
쌓인 미련만큼이나
슬픔으로 다가오는 마음 때문인가보다

태양을 통곡한들
영혼을 찬송한들
경전을 읊은들
아쉬움은 쉽게 사라지질 않는다

새로운 소식을 만난다
또 떠나고 보낸다
모두 그렇게 태어났다

이승의 삶이 영원의 저승으로
이어지는 과정-
단 한 번뿐인 영광의 순간
즐거움, 깨달음, 아쉬움, 사라짐의 순환…

곧 모든 것은 잊혀진다
일상의 자리-현실로 돌아선다
그리고 또 모든 것은 반복된다

슬픔도 그렇게 이어진다

Sorrow comes after sorrow

Everyone is given own life time to live
Each is given own longevity

Now, come a season to end an average span of life,
Also, come a tiding of those passing away, one by one
Be the matter of course for every one, though it may,
It aches one much to think of ones passing away

So much for the various memories left behind by the deceased,
As much for the footprints remembered, big and small,
For all those lingering affections not given up by each departed,
One is unable to let sorrow go

Wailing to the sun for the lost does no good,
Singing for the lost soul,
And reciting scriptures for the lost life,
Do not relieve the sorrow of parting easily

There come another wailing in mourning,
Another leave and is let go,
All came into life just as they did,
All seem to leave just like they do

From this life to the after life,
This process from here to there–
Only one moment of glory
The repetition of joy, enlightenment, regrets, and leaving away

Everything is forgotten soon enough
Everything returns to reality where it all began
Everything repeats itself
Sorrow comes after sorrow.

진실은 부동의 산과 같고 역사는 흐르는 강과 같도다

Ⅵ. 오 오! 대한민국

오 오! 대한민국
O! Korea / Version by, J.C. Son

우리에겐 꿈이 있습니다
This is Our Dream / Version by, J.C. Son

한 여름밤의 소망, 천사여
One Summer Night's Hope, Dear Angel / Version by, J.C. Son

새해를 맞는다
Welcoming the New Year / Version by, J.C. Son

한 시대를 산다
Living a Life of a Time / Version by, J.C. Son

오오! 대한민국

오오! 대한민국!
산은 여전히 여기에 있고
강은 여전히 저편에 흐르네
사계절이 한반도 5000년 역사와 함께 있고
우리의 근대화 100년이, 그리고 나 또한 여기에 함께 있네

오오! 싹 트는 조국,
3 · 1 독립만세(1919) 민족의 근대화 각성이여
8 · 15 광복光復 36년의 치욕에서 해방의 감격이여
8 · 15 건국建國 대한민국, 근대화 물결의 시작이여

오오! 시련 속의 대한민국!
6 · 25 동란; 동족상쟁의 아픔이여, 분단의 고착이여
4 · 19 민주화 운동; 비온 땅-굳어지는 또 하나의 시련이여
5 · 16 군사혁명; 새마을 운동, 근대화 물결-성장의 시동이여

오오! 세계 속의 대한민국!
88 올림픽 성공; 세계는 서울로, 서울은 세계로
97 IMF위기 극복; 금 모으기 정신이여, 재기의 계기여
2002 월드컵 4강; 그 환희와 저력, 붉은 악마의 함성이여

오오! 엄연한 현실, 그리고 미래 속의 대한민국!
통일의 꿈이여?, 화해의 물결이여?
2006; GDP 10위, 국제화 속 우리의 현실-한반도의 생존역학이여,
2019; 근대화-각성 기점, 현대화-국제화 속 100년의 시점이여

진실은 부동의 산과 같고
역사는 흐르는 강과 같도다
삼천리 강산, 한반도 한민족의 새 천년의 앞날에
부강한 발전, 무궁한 영광의 간절한 소망이여!!

O! Korea

O! Korea !
Mountains are still here,
Rivers are still flowing there,
The four seasons keep their course with history-for
five thousand years, And I am also here to stay

O! the waves of modernization of the Korean peninsula
that have budded
3 · 1 The Independence Movement(1919), the awakening
of the nation:
8 · 15 Liberation(1945), the inspiration for the restoration of
independence and 8 · 15. The establishment of Republic of
Korea,
the partition of the Korean peninsula

O! Korea in ordeal …
6 · 25 The Korean War(1950~53): the pain of internal strife:
4 · 19 Democratic reformation: another ordeal: and
5 · 16 Revolution: the wave of Korean modernization and
the New Community Movement

O! Korea in the world…
The Success of the 1988 Olympics, bringing

the world to Korea and Korea to the world
The conquest of the IMF Crisis in 1997,
the spirit of the Gold Donation Movement: and
The semi-finals in the World Cup in 2002,
the rejoicing and the latent power

O! Korea in reality, and in the future…
the pursuit for unification: ?
2006, GDP ranking-10th, Survival Strategies !
The Korean people in 2019, after 100 years of modernization

Truth is an immovable mountain,
History is an ever-flowing river:
Three thousands roads, the dawn of a new millenium,
The eternal glory of the Korean people in the Korean peninsula.

우리에겐 꿈이 있습니다

손에 손에 촛불은
사랑과 소망의 촛불인가요?

우리에겐 내일이 있기에,
젊음이 있기에
미래의 역사에 도약의 꿈을 심습니다

손에 손에 촛불은
사랑과 소망의 촛불인가요?
미움과 무질서의 촛불인가요?

진정, 우리는 꿈을 이루려는 노력에 착실한가요?
진정, 우리는 사회 구성원의 역할에 충실한가요?
진정, 우리는 역사 창조 의지에 의연한가요?

손에 손에 촛불은
사랑과 소망의 촛불인가요?
정의의 횃불인가요?

꿈은 소망을 이루는 욕망을 낳습니다
꿈은 미래의 부강한 나라를 낳습니다

성숙한 시민의식의 촛불이어야-
성화이어야 미래의 역사에
꿈을 이룰 수 있습니다.

우리에겐 꿈이 있습니다

This is Our Dream

Are the candle lights held in hand in hand
for loving and hoping?

Since we have tomorrow,
Because we have our national youth,
We can plant a leaping dream into the future

Are the candle lights held in hand in hand
for loving and hoping?
for hatred, or are they for chaos?

Truly, are we faithful in the effort to get a dream?
Truly, are we going all the way to do our share
as constituents of the society?
Truly, are we resolute in the creation of our history?

Are the candle lights held in hand in hand
for loving and hoping?
Are the torchlight for justice?

A dream bears a hope to have a desire.
A dream bears a prosperous country in our future

Only our mature civic awareness,
for the torch toward a dream,
Can help a glorious dream come true in our history

This is our dream.

한 여름밤의 소망, 천사여

천사여, 이젠
세상에 내려와
함께 살았으면 좋겠다
천사는 누구와도 함께
잘 지낼 수 있지 않니

세상엔 너무 많은 나;
오로지 나만이 선善인 나
오로지 나만이 정의인 나
오로지 나만이 진리인 나
세상엔 너무 많은 너;
너는 나와는 무관한 너
너는 나와는 다른 너
너는 나에겐 중요하지 않은 너

세상엔 너무 많은 이기利己 만이 있다
세상엔 너무 많은 극단極端 만이 있다

우리는 틀림없는
한 지붕 아래 가족, 한 울타리 안 이웃
한 직장의 동료,
한 사회의 파이Pie,
한 시대 속의 백성인데…

천사여, 한 마음 속 높은 곳에 잠재돼 있는
마음이 착한 천사여
이젠 세상에 내려와
함께 살았으면 좋겠다,
보편적 시민과 함께 살았으면 좋겠다
한 여름밤의 소망이여!

One Summer Night's Hope, Dear Angel

My dear angel, now
I hope you come down to this world
and you live with us
Being an angel,
you surely can get along with anyone

In this world,
too many 'I's are there-
the I who thinks only he is good,
the I who thinks only he is just,
the I thinks only he is true,
too many 'You's are there-
the YOU who thinks he has nothing to do with me,
the YOU who thinks he is different from me,
the YOU who thinks I am not important to him
too many egos, too many extremes are there

We are surely families under one roof,
within one fence as neighbors,
co-workers in one place of work,
labors under one management,
a pie in one society,
people in one era, power and patriotic sentiment

My dear angel,
a good hearted angel,
lying dormant at a high place,
deep within one heart
I hope you come down now,
live with us,
live in reality, live in generality
and be my one summer night's hope.

새해를 맞는다

새해를 맞는다
또 하나의 연륜을 만들기 시작하는
새 아침이다

넉넉한 마음이 생겨나는 것은
세상이 온통 대선에 휘둘렸다가
풀린 탓일까

이젠 그만 헐뜯지 말고,
칭찬만 하고 살면 좋겠다
웃는 낯으로
생업의 가치에 몰두하며 살면 좋겠다

태초로부터 오늘까지
오늘로부터 미래의 끝까지
시간은 무한한데
우리는 왜 그리 서둘러 달려 왔을까
생각하며 행동하며 넉넉하게 살면 좋겠다

스스로 만든 틀에 갇혀 살지 말고
하나하나 소프트웨어로 가득 채워
중국도 일본도 부러워할 세상

만들어 가면 좋겠다

몸은 쓸수록 발달하고
머리는 쓸수록 총명해지고
재능은 닦을수록 빛이 난다 하네

새 세상을, 차츰
부강의 열매로 가득 채워가며 살면
참 좋겠다

Welcoming the New Year

The New Year has come
another growth ring is being made
at this new morning

My spirit is so sufficient,
perhaps of the nation
that is just being recovered from
the frenzy of the presidential election

enough of speaking ill of others,
but now speaking well of one another
I wish all praise all others, with smile,
and indulge in our callings worth to live for

From the beginning to today,
from today to the end of the future,
the time is inexhaustible;
then why have we so hurried on with it, I wonder
I wish we all can think, act, and be wholesome in our life

Not being squeezed into the patterns of our own making,
but filling our software with given geniuses one by one,

I wish we can create a nation of ours
to be envied by China and Japan

Using more of our bodies, the better we can develop them;
Using more of our brains, the wiser we become
By cultivating more and deeper,
the genius of men is known to become more brilliant

For the new world, gradually,
I wish we can fill it with fruits
of the rich and the strength we reap.

한 시대를 산다

한 시대를 산다
한 나라를 산다
한 사회를 산다

때로는 무척 불확실한 시대를
때로는 무척 적응하기 힘든 나라를
때로는 무척 부조화의 사회를 산다

세기의 문턱에 서서
삶의 터전, 대한민국의 소박한 백성은
아메바처럼, 애써
무정형無定型의 생존방식으로 살아가야 하나

생생한 것은 의식뿐
삶의 내일이 보다 나은 현실로
다가오길 바라며
삶의 미래가 창조의 역사로
더 진전하길 바라며

일하는 삶 속에
섬기는 나라 속에
하루하루의 주변 속에

내일은
보다 밝은 빛이 비칠 것이라는
확고한 신념을 갖고 살아야지

하나하나
삶은 무한히 소중한 것이기에

Living a Life of a Time

Living a life of a time
Living a life of a country
Living a life of a society

Often, in the time of great uncertainties,
Often, in the country very hard to adapt to,
Often, in the society of great discord

Standing at the threshold of a century
At the site of a given life,
as people of KOREA
Striving for a life as like amoebas,
Must they live a life of amorphous livelihood

The only real is the awareness of
Wishing the life's tomorrow come closer as better reality,
Wishing the future of life to develop
more into a history of a creation

In the life of toil and moil,
In the country to be served,
In the environ of each and every day,

For tomorrow
The brighter light will shine through
With that firm belief they live on

'Cause each and every life
Comes before everything else.

어우러져 아름다운 무지개처럼 어우러져 아름다울 DNA 인간

Ⅶ. 현실은 DNA 갈등

현실은 DNA 갈등
Reality is a DNA discords / Version by, S.G. Hearn

호놀룰루의 물결
Waves of Honolulu / Version by, J.C. Son

인디안 반얀트리
Indian Banyan Tree / Version by, C.Maeng

흑장미 백 송이는
Black Roses / Version by, C.Maeng

액자 속의 동영상
Moving Images in Frame / Version by, J.C. Son

방콕의 어느 하루
One Day in Bangkok / Version by, J.C. Son

현실은 DNA 갈등

잠시 나타났다 사라지는 무지개처럼
잠시 머물고 가는 DNA 흔적
어우러져 아름다운 무지개처럼
어우러져 아름다울 DNA 인간

저마다의 욕망과 이기
너와 나의 생각의 충돌
현실은 온통 DNA 갈등

나날이 다가오는 새로운 물결
변화와 스트레스, 혼돈과 불신
사회는 온통 DNA 경쟁

곳곳에 벌어지는 글로벌 크라이시스
불황과 재해, 분쟁과 패권까지
세상은 온통 DNA 전쟁

내일의 이상은
갈등을 넘어
새로움과 다양성이 공존하는
좋은 형질의 DNA 개발

높은 하늘의 밝은 태양처럼
정의로운, 낮은
하늘의 아름다운 무지개처럼
조화로운 인간 DNA 세상

현실은 DNA 갈등

Reality is a DNA discords

Like a rainbow that appears a little while and soon disappears,
The trace of DNA remain for a while and soon disappear.
Like the rainbow that shows its beauty from joining together,
The human DNA may also be beautiful if joined in harmony

Of one's desires and self-interests,
Of quarrels between your thinking's and mine,
The reality is always engaged in DNA feuds

Day after day, new wave of ideas keeps going,
Come with changes and stresses,
Also confusion and distrust,
The society is then totally engulfed in DNA competitions

All kinds of global crises arise everywhere,
Recessions and disasters, hostilities and power struggles,
Are only a few that the DNA warfare is fought for

But tomorrow's ideals
Leaping over today's conflicts,
Come to develop a good natured DNA,
That lets the world coexist with the new and the diversity

Like the bright sun in the lofty sky,
the day, friendly and warm-hearted,
Makes a world of DNA human in perfect harmony,
Just like the beautiful rainbow hung over in the sky does
Reality is always of DNA discords.

호놀룰루의 물결

호놀룰루 먼 바다의
너울은 태양을 반사한다
황금빛 꿈을 싣는다
넘실넘실
앞바다의 물결로 다가온다
해변의 파도가 된다

화산의 섬(2800년 전)
구전 전승문화의 뿌리
쿡 선장의 발견(1788)
카메하메하 대왕(1795년) 이래
100년간의 킹돔
태평양전쟁(1941)을 거쳐
미 합중국 50번째 주(1959년)가 된다

끊임없이 밀려오는
짜릿한 욕망의 물결들
새로운 기회의 물결들
발등에, 무릎에,
가슴에 부딪친다

파고가 높아지는 세기의 변화들
해변가 온갖 영혼들이
꿈과 현실을 스크램블한다
레크리에이션한다

서핑하는 젊음들에겐
오로지 스릴과 도전만이 있다
야자수 밑에선
훌라춤의 여왕이 낭만을 이끈다
알로하Aloha 하와이
호놀룰루 해변에 서서
꿈과 현실의 물결을 맞는다

Waves of Honolulu

The billows of Honolulu reflect sun lights,
coming from afar off the sea,
along with the golden dreams;
Swaying in, Swaying out-
approaching near,
becoming of many waves of the island
surf into the beach
Island of Hawaii;

Borne by volcanic acts(2800 years ago),
The root of a culture, by an oral tradition
Discovery by Captain Cook(1788),
The 100 year Kingdom
since great King Kamehameha II (1795),
Through the Pacific War(1941),
Became the 50th State of the USA

Without ceasing, The waves of
Honolulu rush upon the shore, and crash
on one's feet, knees, and chest-
The waves of tingling desire,
The waves of new opportunities

The changes of the century rise and fall
as high as the waves;
Crowds of various soul at the beach
scramble their dreams and their realities
and recreate them

For the young surfing waves,
There only exist thrill and challenges;
Under the coconut palm trees
The queen of hula dance romances
onlookers
Aloha, Hawaii,
Standing at the beach of Honolulu,
There, I embrace the waves of dream
and realities.

인디언 반얀 트리

잘 생긴
인디언 반얀-보리수가
여기저기 서 있다

비치 가 공원에도
모아나 호텔 뜰 안에도
인터내셔널 마켓에도
후드 팬트리 뒤뜰에도…
100년이 넘었다는 수종들
허리 둘레가 10미터쯤 됨직하다

상록의 잎새와
그 줄기를 이루는 뭉치가
더욱 신비하게는 에어리얼Aerial 루트로
거대한 우산처럼 펴진 나무를 바치고 서 있다
보이지 않는 땅속의 뿌리도 엄청나리라

식물도감에는
가지마다에서 늘어진 수염 같은 공중뿌리가
땅에 닿는 순간부터 줄기를 이루며
잎새-줄기-뿌리와 흙 속의 수분과
공중의 산소와, 햇빛의 삼자로

이루어지는 자연의 생리-
포토신세시스Photosynthesis-
광합성작용이 일어난다 한다

때때로, 그
큰 그늘 아래 모여드는 사람들로
문화의 공간이 이루어진다

발걸음을 멈추고
줄기 밑둥 틈새마다 박혀 있는
하얀 비둘기 떼를 한 번 더 돌아다본다
낮잠을 자는지…

언젠가는 붓다Buddha가 앉아 해탈解脫했다는
인도의 반얀 보리수도
만나 봐야지…

Indian Banyan Tree

Good looking
Indian Banyan barley trees
stand here and there

In the Park near the beach
in the Moana Hotel yard
at the International Markil
at the Foodpantry back yard
various trees over 100 years old
seem to have 10 meters waists

Evergreen leaves
bundle of stems
as their more mysterious aerial root
sustains to stand the huge trees spreaded like an umbrella
the awful roots hiding in the land

In the botany encyclopedia, I see
aerial roots looking like beards hanging down from each
branches
when it that reaches to the land, it makes stems
leaves, stems, roots and the moisture inside the land
oxygen, sunshines comprise the nature of photosynthesis
luster synthesis occurs

Sometimes,
with the crowds gathered under the tree's shade
it opens a culture space

I stop walking
stuck in each bottom of stems at the trunks
look the white pigeons flock again
wonder if I should take a nap

Sometime in the future, I will visit the Indian Banyan tree
where Buddha sits and enters into nirvana
Indian Banyan tree
plan to visit.

흑장미 백 송이는

아내 생일의
흑장미 백 송이는
사나흘이 멀다하고 고개 숙이는데

옆자리
서양란은
서너 달이 넘도록
보라색 한껏 뽐내고 있네

한자리 건너
동양란은
예닐 곱 달은 지난 듯한데
꽃향기 가득히 마냥 청초하네

창가
선인장은
해를 두세 번은 넘긴 듯한데
가끔
긴 여행에서 돌아와
물을 듬뿍 주면
시들었나 싶었던 잎
다시 싱싱해 지네

신비하도다
한 환경 속
꽃마다의 개성이여
생명력이여

백화百花 쟁爭이여

Black Roses

It is my wife's birthday
one hundred black roses
faded every three days

Beside,
western roses
even over three months
are in full blossoms in violet color

Right next to it
oriental roses
looked as if six-seven months passed
neat in full perfume
the window cactus
looked as if two or three years passed

Sometimes
when I come back from long trip
I supply water fully,
the fading leaves
become fresh again

Mysterious!
In one circumstance
I see the individuality of each flower
and its long life!

A Hundred flowers battle!

액자 속의 동영상

- 코나 미팅 -

대양大洋 한복판에
공룡처럼 솟아오른 시커먼 화산섬
아직도
정상에 붉은 용암을 내뿜는 분화구가 있다

자본가들이 만들어 놓은
리조트와 클럽과 비행장은
열선처럼 연결되는 동선을 타고
곳곳에서 모여드는 회원들의 레저와
모임과 만남을 겸하기엔 자못 낭만적인 곳
동반되는 가족들과 반가움의 인사가 바쁘다

원생대原生代의 고장에서…
오전마다
수술 환자들의 이슈Issue를 놓고
열띤 토론을 한다
오후엔 곳곳의 명소를 찾는다
역사박물관이며, 마을 교회며,
냄새 구수한 특산물-
코나 커피의 산지들을 찾는다
더러는 피트니스를 나선다

어느덧, 아쉬움의 일정이 다가오면,
고장의 명물
폴리네이션 횃불 춤-
루아우Luau 파티가 절정을 이룬다
프로들의 망중한忙中閑은
커리어career를 증진시킨다
아쉬움의 이별 인사를 나눈다

잠시 눈을 감고, 저마다의 삶 속의 일정을
액자 속의 동영상에 담아본다

-이 글을 Dr. Rainer(W.Gerald) 교수님께 드립니다.

Moving Images in Frame

-Kona Meeting-

In the middle of the Ocean,
a deep black volcanic island stands,
rising above waters as if a dragon is gushing up.
Even now, on its summit
is the living crater that vomits red lava
Here are resorts built by investors;
also are here the clubs, shopping centers, and an airport
Members gather from all corner's of the globe
coming through the ridge that beams like a heat wave
Here, the familiar faces and joyful families reunite together

At a place born of earth's crust changes in the Proterozoic Period,
debates are quietly unfold,
on how to operate on patients, on survival rates,
and on the environment of medical treatments
Though romantically contrasting,
the afternoon half of the days
have been filled with visits to native history museums,
and the visits to Kona-coffee growing districts,
the savory principal product growers

In the evening, the Luau party,
thrown together with Polynesian torchlight dance
is the gem of the whole event
Before long,
the sorrow of parting awaits near,
prompting all into sharing busy farewell words
For these professionals,
the leisure out of their busy schedule
gives a boost in their career

In a moment,
closing my eyes,
I fill these moving images in my frame.

-Remembering Dr. Rainer W. Gerald.

방콕의 어느 하루

여행지, 방콕의 어느 하루,
출라롱콘Chulalongkorn대학의
한 작은 강당에선
특이한 모임이 열리고 있다
해피니스Happiness가 그 주제,
다양한 문화들이 교차하는 곳에선
새로운 이슈들이 솟아나게 마련이다
단상 단하의 눈빛들이 차분해 보인다
왕정 체제 하의 이곳 태국, 특히 방콕은
산업화, 민주화, 세계화로 가는 길목에서-
불교적 가치와 유교적 철학의 혼재 속에서-
정보화, 과학화의 동서양의 문물이
노도처럼 흘러들어오는 역사의 흐름에서-
생존을 위한 생물학적 욕구와 갈등을
심신의 조화 속에
행복지수, 웰빙 지수를 꼽아보려는
시도는 당연해 보인다
세상의 여기저기,
현 세기인世紀人들이 한결같이 추구하는
궁극적 고지는 마음의 평화,
영적 '해피니스' …
여기 한 대학의 작은 강당에 모여

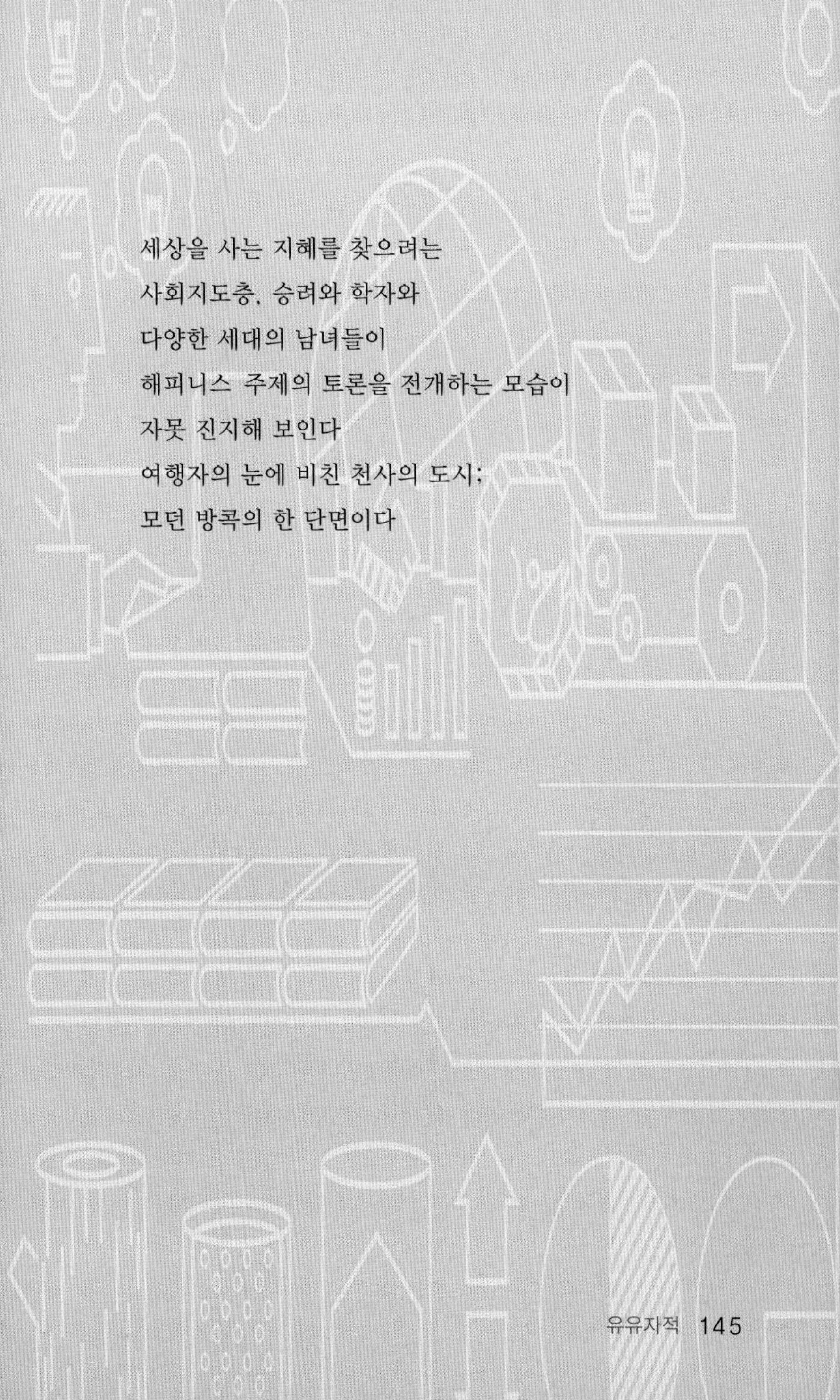

세상을 사는 지혜를 찾으려는
사회지도층, 승려와 학자와
다양한 세대의 남녀들이
해피니스 주제의 토론을 전개하는 모습이
자못 진지해 보인다
여행자의 눈에 비친 천사의 도시;
모던 방콕의 한 단면이다

One day in Bangkok

One day in Bangkok
a destination of a traveler,
at a small auditorium of Chulalongkorn University,
a unique meeting is being held
The main topic is happiness
Cause many different cultures intersect here,
new issues are bound to spring up afresh
All eyes,
whether of one up on the platform
or those on the floor, are composed quietly
In Thailand,
under the kingly rule,
especially in Bangkok-
at the crossroad of industrialization, democratization,
and globalization-
in the mingle of the value of Buddhism, Islamic
and Confucian ideas-
in the flow of a history
into which all sorts of information, science,
and various Occidental and Western cultures
flow in like roaring waves-
it seems fair and proper for the subjects

to count on the numbers
for their happiness and well-being,
and to seek biological desires and conflicts
for their survival
in the harmony of body and soul
May it be defind as the spiritual 'Happiness'
Here, gathered at a small auditorium,
seeking for the wisdom to live on the planet earth,
are the social leaders, monks, scholars,
and all generations of man and women
Their appearances look much sincere
This is one phase of life of modern Bangkok, a City of Angel,
impressed on the eyes of a traveler.

손이여 아쉬움 걷어내고 변해가는
새 제주의 새 모습을 사랑만 하옵소서

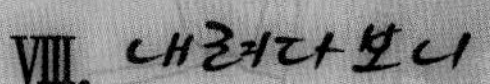

Ⅷ. 내려다보니

내려다보니
Looking Back / Version by, J.W. Chung

강화로 가는 길은
The Pass to Gang-Wha / Version by, J.C. Son

제주의 하룻밤을 잠 못 이루네
The Night in Jeju / Version by, J.C. Son

선셋 앤 선라이즈
Sunset and Sunrise / Version by, S.G. Hearn

내려다보니

내려다보니
둘이서
처음엔
철 침대 하나가 좁지 않더니
아들이
하나, 둘, 셋,
온돌방 둘, 셋이 비좁더니
일하며 살며
넓히는 동안에
첫째, 둘째, 그리고 막내까지
짝을 지어 나가니
방마다 따로따로 넓더니
어느새
마주 보고 자자고
잡아다니니
다시 하나면
족하네

Looking back

Looking back
For the two of us
At first
A small Iron bed was enough
And then came
The first,
the second, and the youngest son
Even two or three rooms became crammed
While we were working and living
On getting a bigger space,
The first, the second,
And even the youngest
Left us with their loved ones
And every room became to big
In no time at all,
Wanting to go to sleep
while watching each other's eye,
Pulled each other closer
One bed
Was once more enough for the two of us.

강화로 가는 길은

강화로 가는 길은
코스모스 길

세 아들, 아내와 함께
무릎 위에 도시락 펼쳐놓으면
한주일이 곽 차는 주말이었다

황금색 벼 물결 속
하늘을 바라보고 벌렁 누우면
가을이 꽉 차는 주말이었다

마니산 돌계단 길
밀며 당기며 기어오르면
가슴이 꽉 차는 주말이었다

아련히 떠오르는
새마을 노래 시절
꿈으로 꽉 차던 시절

강화로 가는 길은
코스모스 길

The Pass to Gang-Hwa

The pass to Gang-Hwa, was
A pass by cosmos blossoms

Three sons and wife
opened their lunch basket
on their knees;
Used to make our weekends
close with full gaieties

Among waves of golden rice plants,
I used to lie down on my back;
As I look up to the sky,
the end of the week was near
on a full of autumn tints

On stony stairway to the Mani San
We used to go up at a crawl,
the end of the week was
full of the chest

Though, I trace back in dim memory,
The 'Age of New Village Song'
Full of dream
were we all

The pass to Gang-Hwa,
The pass with sweet scent of cosmoses.

제주의 하룻밤을 잠 못 이루네

태고太古로 이어지는
제주의 하룻밤을 잠 못 이루네
한라 영봉, 삼다삼무 三多三無
옛 신비 추억 속에 잠 못 이루네

오름과 오름 사이 구름이 춤추던 곳
숲과 숲 사이 노루가 뛰던 곳
계곡과 계곡 사이 무지개 서던 곳
파도와 파도 사이 해녀가 숨쉬던 곳

하늘길 바닷길로
근대화 바람 타네
글로벌 사이버Cyber 길로
현대화 물결 타네
옛 것이 새 것 되네
비바람 하루방 땅 이상향 되어가네

손이여
아쉬움 걷어내고
변해가는 새 제주의
새 모습을
사랑만 하옵소서

미래로 이어지는
제주의 하룻밤을 한(큰)꿈 이루소서

The Night at Jeju

The night at Jeju
Yearns back to ancient times
I cannot go back to sleep

The sacred mountain Halla
Of Sam-Da Sam-Mu
In those mysterious
Memoirs in time of refuge
I cannot go back to sleep

Between Oreum and Oreum, where clouds dance
Between forest and forest, where deer skip about
Between valley and valley, where rainbow showed
Between wave and wave, where Haenyo(women divers) breathe

Within modern stream
Sky roads, sea roads, cyber roads,
The old becomes the new
The land of rainy wind becomes paradise

Visitor,
Now forget regret
Just love
New nature
Those ever-changing new Jeju

Please go back to sleep at down,
(With a big dream).

선셋 앤 선라이즈

석양夕陽이 수평선 너머로
가라앉는 순간 순간
붉게 물드는 바다 -
파도는 계속 해안에 철썩인다

말이 적은 남성들, 말이 빠른 엄마들 속에
인터넷 TV를 껴안고 킬킬 대던 꼬마는
어느새 쑥쑥 엄마의 어깨를 넘는다
뮤직에 열중이더니 이번엔
페인팅의 재능을 과시한다

오브제 - '선셋 인 파라다이스Sunset in Paradise' 를
모네Monet처럼 그렸단다
딸의 첫 작품에
절대가격을 제시하고 사인Sign을 받아낸다

명인名人의 별미 - 만찬에 이어
코나Kona커피의 향기를 손에 들고
야자수 잎 나부끼는 훈풍 속
밤하늘 별들의 바다로 발걸음을 옮긴다

손에 잡힐 듯 이름 붙은 큰 별들과
더 멀리 흩어져 반짝이는 은하수銀河水 성운星雲을
쳐다보노라면
오 오 바로 지금, 이곳이
하늘과 땅과 바람과 바다가 만드는
순간 순간의 파라다이스

밤새 흐르는 시간,
현실과 꿈속을 오가는 동영상
새벽에 다시 만날 생명들에게 빛을 비춰주기 위하여
이 밤에도 에너지를 충전시키며 돌고 있을
그 태양 -
우주의 신비 - 대칭對稱/Symmetry의 원리이다

선셋 앤 선라이즈 Sunset and Sunrise !!

Sunset and Sunrise

At an instant moment
The setting sun is
Submerging o'er the sea horizon
The sea turns red –
But the waves are still bellowing

Amid the men of quietness and of the loquacious women
A giggling youngster with her lap-top internet
Suddenly, furtibly looking over mom's shoulder
Enthused in music a moment prior, and now
Ostentatiously shows off her gift in painting

Claiming that
She painted Object's "Sunset in Paradise" like Monet
Upon an absolute price, had me signed on a contract

Following an exquisite dinner extraordinair, and
Kona coffee and it's aroma in hand
Moving our gaits into the seashore under the stars of night

Gazing up the seemingly touchable popular stars and
The Galaxy and the Nebulae twinkling far, far away,

Ah, yes, here and now, the sky and the earth,
the wind and the sea are
Creating paradises moment by moment

Elapsing time throughout all night,
The reflexes go to and fro, betwixt the reality and the dream,
For the lives that come across one-another in the early dawn,
The sun energizes the driving power even this night revolving,
The mystery of the universe – the symmetrical theory.

나의 소중한 분들에게 퇴임인사 드립니다

이제 2001년 8월
의업 43년과의 만남;
공군 군의관, 서울의대, 백병원, 그리고 최근의 직장
정든 이곳 서울중앙병원-
AMC, 아산병원 및 울산의대 10년의 인연들;
소중한 사람들과 임상, 교육, 연구의 현장에서,

함께 일해온 위아래 동료 모든 분들께는 크나큰 고마움을,
큰 병으로 수술 받은 모든 환자들께는 쾌유를 소망하면서
이제 퇴임하는 헤어짐의 인사를 드립니다.

외과적 질병의 진단 및 수술 적응, 병소의 완전 절제
창상치유와 조기회복, 만기이환율의 예측과 예방
그리고 장기 무병생존의 결과를 추구하며
일진월보하는 의학의 길에서,
임상과 수련, 교육과 연구를 함께 해온 나날들,

외과, 흉부외과 영역- 폐 외과, 폐암외과의 세부영역에서
확립된 이론의 개체별 적응에 얼마나 오랜 경험의 성숙이,
질병별 임상 실제의 문제 해결에
얼마나 다양한 전문성의 기여가 요했는지를…

외과는 그래서, 때로는 무대 위의 예술이요 창작이라는
착각으로 즐겨왔습니다.

유구한 한강의 흐름을 바라보며
갈수록 태산인 우리의 역사, 카오스의 미래
동고동락해 온 우리 사회 속의 의료를 돌아보며
파이의 한 조각의 역할에 최선을 다했노라
마음 속에 간직한 채

이제 보편적 시민으로,
새로운 세기 속에, 새 천지 속에, 희망을 안고
인류가 쌓아온 지혜의 들판에 함께 어울려, 자유로운 마음으로
나만의 꿈과 사랑과 진실의 열매를 익히렵니다.
우리 모두 함께 사는 세상,
보다 바람직한 내일이기를 바라며…
백사여의百事如意 장수무량長壽無量하시기 바랍니다.

50주년 재상봉의 인사

탄생誕生의 인연으로
한 울타리에서 배움을 함께 하더니
졸업장과 면허증을 받아들고
벅찬 가슴으로 세상을 맞더니
어느새 50년이란 세월이
눈 깜짝할 사이에 흘러갔습니다.

2008년…

그간 걸어온 길이 얼마나 즐거웠습니까?
헤엄쳐 온 바다가 얼마나 험하였습니까?
소망하던 꿈이 얼마나 이루어졌습니까?

의학의 원리Principle를 터득하고
임상의 실제Practice를 다스리고
환자의 생명을 지키기 위하여

긴 수련의 과정을, 진료의 복잡함을,
연구의 어려움을 마다않고 불철주야로
젊음의 정열을 다하여 왔습니다.

영광으로만 가득하지 아니하였을 지라도,
때로는 야속하리만큼의 의료 환경이었을 지라도,

때로는 삶의 순간들이 가시방석 같았을 지라도
오로지 우리들의 보람이었습니다.

오늘의 몸과, 마음과, 영혼을 있게 해주신 하늘에 대하여,
삶의 터전을 있게 해주신 환자와 사회와 학문에 대하여,
조상과, 스승과 그리고
소중한 우리들의 우정에 대하여
감사하지 않을 수 없음 입니다.

50주년을 맞이하여 서로 멀리서 지내온 우리
한 · 미 동문 모두가
오랜 세월 삶을 동반해온 아내들과 함께
우리들의 모교와 시계탑 앞에서 만나
팔도강산의 끝 남쪽바다로 함께 떠나보시지 않으시렵니까?

에필로그

I

가끔 조용한 호숫가에 앉아 작은 돌을 호수 한복판으로 던져본다. 금세 중심中心 원圓에 이어 다음다음 여러 개의 넓은 원이 밖으로 밖으로 퍼져간다. 점점 낮은 파고波高로 넓게 이어져간다. 그리고 평탄한 수면水面으로 돌아간다.
세상사世上事에 대한 삶들의 관심처럼…

II

한글로 적어본 글;
그대 걸어온 발자국 / 모래 위에 남긴 발자국 / 파도는 쉽게 지워버리네.
그대 걸어갈 발자국 / 미래 속에 남길 발자국 / 세상은 쉽게 변해버리네 / 의 주어主語; 그대Thy를 우리로,
우리 걸어온 발자국 / 생활 속에 남긴 발자국 / 사람은 쉽게 잊어버리네 / 우리 영혼 속에 새겨질 발자국 / 꿈과 사랑과 진실의 발자국 / 영원히 간직할 우리들의 발자국
무리일까?

III

영문 버전version을 시도해 보았다.
같은 한글 원문原文에 대한 A와 B의 두 개성, 두 개의 언어로. "동서 문화권의 언어로 번역 하기란 쉽지 않지요" 라던 MGH의 Dr. Grillo(Hermes C.)교수의 말씀을 기억한다.
'교수님의 사랑을 오래오래 기억하렵니다'
읽는 이의 문화 인식, 번역하는 개성이 서로 같을 수 없기 때문이다. 생각an idea, a concet의 공감을 스펀지sponge화化하면 관념의 다양화는 계절처럼 변화의 과정으로 이어지리라.

IV

관심의 '키 워드' 들을 내일 모레의 새로운 이슈들로 전개해 나가 보자;
IT, 시간, 스페이스의 빅 데이터Big Data들을 넘어, 일인일기一人一技하는 무의식 속의 세계화로 빅뱅Big Bang 해 나가면, 저마다의 유전자가 다 고유하니, 국경 없는 자연과 환경, 여행과 취미, 언어와 종교의 자유 속에서 웰빙Wellbeing을 향한 간절한 마음들로 이어지는 창의의 열매는 무궁무진하리라.

Epilogue

I

Sitting by a tranquil lake.
I throw a small stone towards the middle of the water.
Soon a small circle appears
And then
Surrounded by many larger circles.
Continued by lower waves
Extending larger and larger.
And then, water returns to an even surface
Like life's interest in worldly affairs.

II

Writing in korean:
"Thou" whose footsteps / footsteps left on the beach /
Are easily erased by wave.
"Thou" whose footsteps / footsteps in the future /
Are easily changed by life. Replace the subject
"Thou" to "We" :
"We" whose footsteps / footsteps left in life /
Are easily forgotten.
"We whose footsteps of the soul /
Footsteps of dreams, love and truth / footsteps that will last forever.
What a change. Could I convert a poem? Or is it too much to ask?

III

I attempt an English translation in poetry.
One can see the difference in character between A and B from the Korean version.
I remember, "it is not easy to translate between different cultures and languages of East and West."
Said Professor Grillo(Hermes C.) MGH, Boston.
"I Love You Dr. Grillo!"
The readers' culture and character of translation cannot all be the same.
If one appreciates and absorbs an idea and a concept like sponge,
Distant understandings can under go a process of change like seasonal change.

IV

Let us develop 'keywords of interest' into new issues for our day after tomorrow;
Beyond IT, Time, and Big Data from Space.
Let us, with one man, one skill, Big Bang ourselves (in our subconscious world).
Then, since man has an inherent gene,
And with borderless nature and environment, freedom of travel and pastime, language and knowledge.
And with sincere wish for man's well-being.
The fruit of originality will be infinite.